THE CEASING OF NOTIONS

The Ceasing of Notions

AN EARLY ZEN TEXT
FROM THE DUNHUANG CAVES

With Selected Comments by
Soko Morinaga Roshi

and an Introduction by
Martin Collcutt

Translated into German
by Ursula Jarand;
into English by
Venerable Myokyo-ni
and Michelle Bromley

WISDOM PUBLICATIONS • BOSTON

IN ASSOCIATION WITH THE ZEN TRUST
AND THE BUDDHIST SOCIETY • LONDON

Wisdom Publications
199 Elm Street
Somerville, MA 02144 USA
www.wisdompubs.org

First Published by The Zen Trust, 1988, as "A Treatise on the Ceasing of Notions."
Published in association with the Buddhist Society, London.

Library of Congress Cataloging-in-Publication Data

Bodhidharma, 6th cent.
  [Jue guan lun. English]
  The Ceasing of notions : an early Zen text from the Dunhuang Caves / with
selected comments by Soko Morinaga Roshi and an introduction by Martin Collcutt
; translated into German by Ursula Jarand, into English by Venerable Myokyo-ni and
Michelle Bromley.
      pages cm
  Includes bibliographical references.
  ISBN 1-61429-041-5 (pbk. : alk. paper)
  1. Zen Buddhism—Doctrines—Early works to 1800. 2. Bodhidharma, 6th cent. Jue
guan lun. I. Morinaga, Soko, 1925–1995, writer of added commentary. II. Collcutt, Martin, 1939– writer of added commentary. III. Jarand, Ursula, translator. IV. Myokyo-ni,
translator. V. Morinaga, Soko, 1925–1995. Novice to master. Selections. 2013. VI. Title.
  BQ9299.B624C4813 2013
  294.3'85—dc23

                            2012020570

ISBN 9781614290414   eBook ISBN 9781614290452

16 15 14 13 12   5 4 3 2 1

Cover design by Phil Pascuzzo. Interior design by Gopa & Ted2, Inc. Set in ITC Galliard.

Printed in the United States of America.

Table of Contents

Introduction

THE ORIGINAL TEXT AND
THE TRANSLATION

T*HE CEASING OF NOTIONS* is the title given to the translation of one of the Chinese texts from Dunhuang, which are called the *Jue-guan lun* in Chinese and *Zekkanron* in Japanese. The vast caves near Dunhuang, an oasis on the ancient Silk Road in the Gansu province of western China, also known as the Mogao Caves and the Caves of the Thousand Buddhas, comprised a network of 492 ancient temples. From the fourth until the fourteenth century, Buddhist monks at Dunhuang—who used the remote caves as places for prayer and meditation in their search for enlightenment—collected scriptures, sacred paintings, and statues from western Asia and Tibet. Pilgrims passing through the area painted murals covering some four hundred and fifty thousand square feet inside the caves. Construction of the Buddhist cave shrines began around 366 CE as places to store scriptures and works of art. The caves thus came to serve as repositories for thousands of sacred texts and to contain some of the finest examples of early Buddhist art spanning a period of a thousand years.

Sometime after the eleventh century, some of the caves were walled off and used as storehouses for used and damaged manuscripts and religious objects. They remained virtually unknown until the early twentieth century. Then, in the early 1900s, a Chinese Daoist named Wang Yuanlu, who was acting as the guardian of some of these cave temples, discovered a walled-up area beside a corridor leading to a main cave. Behind the wall was a small cave stuffed with an enormous hoard of manuscripts and paintings on hemp, silk, or paper dating from 406 to 1002 CE. These included ancient Buddhist texts in Chinese and other Asian languages. Among them were several manuscript copies of the text offered here as *The Ceasing of Notions*.

Around 1907, Wang Yuanlu sold many of the ancient scrolls to Western travelers exploring the Silk Road, including Sir Aurel Stein and Paul Pelliot, who eagerly acquired these rare Buddhist texts and carried them back to Europe. The Japanese Buddhist scholars D. T. Suzuki and Kuno Horyu, among others, seem to have rediscovered copies of the text in Pelliot's collection in the early 1930s.

Discussing, as it does, the path to enlightenment, this text has long had an important place in Chinese and Japanese Zen thought and practice. This text has also been partially translated into English by John R. McRae in his illuminating essay "The Ox-head School of Chinese Ch'an Buddhism: From Early Ch'an to the Golden Age."[1] McRae's essay is a valuable study of the Ox-head school of early Chinese Chan (Zen) from which the *Jue-*

guan lun seems to have emerged. McRae discusses problems of establishing the text and its authorship; it has been variously attributed to Bodhidharma, Shen Hui, the legendary Ox-head school founder Niutou Farong, or—most likely perhaps—a later anonymous member of the school sometime during the late eighth century.[2] The Japanese version of the ancient text has been translated into German under the title *Dialog über das Auslöschen der Anschauung* by Ursula Jarand, abbess of the Zen monastery Daishuin West in northern California.[3] Ursula practiced Zen in Kyoto under the guidance of Soko Morinaga Roshi for many years. Her German translation, like this one, incorporates a Japanese commentary on the text by Soko Morinaga Roshi.

Venerable Myokyo-ni, who founded the Zen Centre in London on her return from training at Daitokuji in Kyoto, where she met Soko Morinaga Roshi, felt a strong affinity with this text. She recognized its importance and the value of Morinaga Roshi's commentary as a training aid for Zen students. Therefore this present translation, made by the Venerable Myokyo-ni and Michelle Bromley, takes into account earlier German, English, and Japanese translations but places more emphasis on accessibility and helpfulness to readers who are practicing Zen, or interested in Zen, than on severe literalness or heavy scholarly apparatus. To this end, the title of the Chinese text translated rather abstractly by one scholar as *A Dialogue on the Contemplation Extinguished* and by McRae as *A Treatise on the Transcendence of Cognition* is rendered simply as *The Ceasing of Notions*, which is both close to the spirit of the original Chinese title, *Jue-guan lun*, and expressive of the central Buddhist and Zen issue discussed throughout the text, namely the shedding of the delusions and notions that veil the truth of immanent buddhahood. In the interests of accessibility, too, Chinese Chan terms and personalities are given in their Japanese readings. Moreover, the Japanese terms are presented as simply as possible to Western readers; macrons are not used to distinguish long vowel sounds in Japanese. Readers who are looking for an academic discussion of the *Jue-guan lun* text and its relation to the development of early Chan should refer to the McRae article or scholarly treatments and textual studies by Tokiwa and others.[4]

The *Jue-guan lun* (*The Ceasing of Notions*) in its earliest form was a series of brief questions about the practice of the Buddhist Way and the attainment of understanding by a novice, known in Japanese as Emmon and in Chinese as Yuanmen, and the responses by his teacher, the monk known in Japanese as Nyuri and in Chinese as Ruli. Emmon's questions express or reveal his clinging to "notions" of "delusions" about the Way and the attainment of true understanding. Nyuri's answers, often enigmatic, are intended to encourage Emmon to shed his notions and recognize the truth of his buddhahood, which has always been his, if he would only see it. Because the questions and answers are often terse and their full implications difficult for a reader to grasp, it is very helpful to have the straightforward, insightful commentary provided here by Soko Morinaga Roshi.

THE ZEN LITERATURE OF
QUESTION, ANSWER, AND COMMENTARY

As readers respond to the challenges of Emmon's questions, ponder the implications of Nyuri's responses, and reflect on the wider understanding provided by Morinaga Roshi's comments, they will quickly realize that this text, in its original form, and with the added commentary by Morinaga Roshi, is an early example of a form of "question and answer" literature, and of a "literature of commentary," that has played such an important role in the transmission of Buddhist teaching, and especially of Zen Buddhism. I am thinking here of the various collections of Zen "cases" known as *koans* (*gong-an*) and the commentaries on those koans that have come down to us. In some texts the commentary was in the form of a verse. These cases and the comments on them have served to make lay, as well as monastic, practitioners ponder the meaning of their lives and their search for understanding through Buddhism, and Zen, and they have helped to keep the tradition alive, accessible, and expansive over time.

The most famous of these koan/commentary collections are the Song dynasty Chinese collections: the *Blue Cliff Record* (in Chinese *Biyan-lu*, in Japanese *Hekiganroku*) compiled by master Yuanwu Keqin (Engo Kokugon in Japanese) and the *Gateless Gate* (in Chinese *Wumenguan*, in Japanese *Mumonkan*) composed in 1228 by the Chinese Chan master Wumen Huikai (in Japanese, Mumon Ekai; 1183–1260).[5]

Japanese monks like Eisai (1141–1215) and Dogen (1200–1253), who practiced Zen in China in the late twelfth and thirteenth centuries, brought some of these koan collections back to Japan; they were used by the many Chinese Zen masters who came to Japan in the thirteenth and early fourteenth centuries and helped to establish the Rinzai transmission of Zen as a vibrant expression of Buddhism in Japan. Dogen, who established the Soto tradition of Zen in Japan, is sometimes said to have rejected koan study in favor of purely practicing *shikantaza*, or "just sitting"—but in his writings he frequently included koans from the old Chinese collections, and, in some cases, added his own commentary to them. As William Bodiford points out in his *Soto Zen in Medieval Japan*, Dogen used more than 580 koans in his teachings. In the *Kana Shobogenzo*, Dogen elaborates on 55 koans, quoting them in their entirety, and he refers to some of them more than 280 times.[6] Later, in the mid-Tokugawa period, two of the greatest Zen masters of early modern Japan, Hakuin Ekaku of the Rinzai school of Zen (1685–1768) and Tenkei Denson of the Soto sect of Zen (1648–1735), wrote commentaries on the Blue Cliff Record.[7]

SOKO MORINAGA ROSHI

The very accessible and helpful commentary on *The Ceasing of Notions* provided in this volume was added by Soko Morinaga Roshi (1925–1995), one of the most revered Japanese Rinzai Zen masters of his generation, and one who has trained American and European as well as Japanese students of Zen. And, as we have seen, Morinaga Roshi's commentary may be placed in a long and distinguished tradition of Zen questioning and commentary regarding the self and the search for true self-understanding.

As a young man Morinaga Roshi found himself adrift and unsure of what he really wanted to do in post–World War II Japanese society. Drawn to Zen practice, he decided to become a Zen monk in Kyoto. He began his Zen training in his early twenties, in 1948, at Daitokuji under Goto Zuigan (1879–1965), formerly abbot of the Rinzai Zen monastery of Myoshinji and at that time abbot of Daitokuji. Morinaga trained and practiced at the monastery of Daitokuji from 1949 to 1963, becoming the head monk in the monk's hall. He was the Dharma successor to Oda Sesso Roshi (1901–1966), a disciple of Goto Zuigan, who succeeded Zuigan as abbot of Daitokuji.

In 1965 Morinaga Roshi assumed the abbacy of the monastery of Daishuin in Kyoto. Daishuin was a small community of six or seven monk-disciples living a Zen life with their teacher. At Daishuin, Roshi built a Zen meditation hall that was open to laypeople in the area, including foreign students. On Sundays he gave talks on Zen, teisho or Dharma lectures, at Daishuin, which were also open to lay visitors. In these teisho he might use classic Zen texts such as the Platform Sutra, but his talks were always down-to-earth and directed at bringing Zen understanding into the lives and experiences of his listeners. Daishuin was a subtemple of the much larger Myoshinji, and Morinaga Roshi was for many years the monks' hall roshi for the Myoshinji monks. He went on to serve as the president of Hanazono University in Kyoto, the primary training university of the Rinzai School in Japan. As his reputation as a Zen master grew within Japan, he traveled to Hokkaido and other parts of the country to lead meditation retreats for monks and laypeople.

Morinaga Roshi had a number of Western students, among them Thomas Minick (Shaku Daijo) and Ursula Jarand (Myotsu Daishi), both students of his for many years at Daishuin. Shaku Daijo was ordained there as a Zen monk in 1979. Thomas and Ursula were married by Roshi, then came to the United States, and together planned and built Daishuin West in Humboldt County in northern California, which was inaugurated in 1996 as a Western counterpart to Daishuin in Kyoto and is a Zen temple in the Myoshinji line. Morinaga Roshi did not live to attend the opening ceremony of Daishuin West, but he did see and approve the plans for the monastery before his death.

Roshi also made annual visits of several weeks each summer to England to lead Zen practice and lecture on selected Zen texts at the Buddhist Society's annual summer schools. In this he was responding to an invitation from the Venerable Myokyo-ni, whom he had known for many years. Myokyo-ni had practiced Zen at Daitokuji for twelve years from 1960 under Oda Sesso Roshi and, after his death, under his successor Sojun Kannun. Morinaga was also in training at Daitokuji and serving as the head monk there.

Several of Morinaga Roshi's books and essays on Zen have been translated into German and English. Now out of print, *Pointers to Insight: Life of a Zen Monk*, which draws on his own experiences as a monk searching for insight, was published in 1985 by the Zen Centre, London. In a somewhat different form, this material was translated by Belenda Attaway Yamakawa and published in 2002 as *Novice to Master: An Ongoing Lesson in the Extent of My Own Stupidity*. Three years later Ursula Jarand's German translation of the *Zekkanron*, with Morinaga Roshi's commentary, was translated into English by Myokyo-ni and Michelle Bromley and published by the Zen Centre as *A Treatise on the Ceasing of Notions: An Early Text from Tun-huang*.

Each of these books presents Zen thought and practice in a very direct and stimulating way. *Novice to Master*, for example, which draws on the experiences of his own severe training in Zen and his life as a teacher, opens with a section devoted to his experiences and perceptions as a novice monk: "The prospect of my own death." In his characteristically direct and challenging way, Roshi goes to the heart of things in the introduction to *Novice to Master*.

If I were to sum up the past forty years of my life, the time since I became a monk, I would have to say that it has been an ongoing lesson in the extent of my own stupidity. When I speak of my stupidity, I do not refer to something that is innate, but rather to the false impressions that I have cleverly stockpiled, layer upon layer, in my imagination.

Whenever I travel to foreign countries to speak, I am invariably asked to focus on one central issue: Just what is satori, just what is enlightenment? This thing called satori, however, is a state that one can understand only through experience. It cannot be grasped or explained through words alone.

By way of example, there is a proverb that says, "To have a child is to know the heart of a parent." Regardless of how a parent may demonstrate the parental mind to a child, that child cannot completely understand it. Only when children become parents themselves do they fully know the heart of a parent. Such an understanding can be likened to enlightenment, although enlightenment is far deeper still.

"The purpose of practice," writes Morinaga, "is not to increase knowledge but to scrape the scales off the eyes, to pull the plugs out of the ears. Through practice one comes to see reality. And although it is said that 'no medicine can cure fully,' whatever prompts me to realize 'I was a fool' is, in fact, just such a medicine."

MORINAGA ROSHI'S COMMENTARY ON
The Ceasing of Notions

Let us now look more closely at the text of, and Mori-naga Roshi's commentary on, *The Ceasing of Notions.* Here, using one or two examples, I will try to point out some of the ways in which Morinaga makes this elu-sive ancient text accessible to readers who, like Emmon, have many questions to ask about their own search for the Way of the Buddha and their possible attainment of enlightenment.

The Ceasing of Notions is clearly intended as a practi-cal straightforward translation of, and guide to, an early Zen text that crystallizes many of the essentials of Zen thought, and one that is as relevant now as it was in Tang dynasty China. The work itself is in the form of a dialogue or series of questions and answers between two imaginary figures: Master Nyuri and his disciple Emmon.

Although the original Chinese text is undivided, the Japanese editors have divided it into fifteen sections. This division is followed in this English translation of *The Ceasing of Notions.* Each section clusters questions and answers around a principal topic. Section I, for instance, deals with the central question of finding the Great Way of the Buddha and pacifying the heart (or, as it was translated by McRae, the mind—the Chinese character *xin* is the heart, moral nature, the mind, the affections, and the intention, but it is translated here as *heart* throughout):

1a The Great Way is without limit, fathomless and
    subtle, beyond comprehension, beyond words.
       Master Nyuri (whose name means "Entrance
    into the Principle") and his disciple Emmon
    ("Gate of Affinities") discuss the truth.

The enlightened Zen master Nyuri is guiding his disciple Emmon in his search for self-understanding. Their
conversation opens with Nyuri's presentation of the
Great Way (of the truth of the universe) as "without
limit, fathomless and subtle, beyond comprehension,
beyond words."

In his comment Roshi discusses *fathomless and subtle*
by raising the issue of causation in Buddhism, expressed
in the Japanese term *innen*, which he explains in terms
of its two constituent characters: *in*, "inner cause," and
en, the factors contributing to that cause. And then, to
clarify this rather abstruse distinction, he introduces the
analogy of a bell in which the ability to make sound is
its *in* and the factors contributing to that sound—the
clapper, the metal, the size of the bell, etc.—are the *en*.
And when they meet the sound of the bell is manifest.

Just as Master Nyuri uses "skillful means" to shake
Emmon out of his confusion and into self-awakening,
so the Roshi too uses skillful means to clarify the text,
and its true meaning, for his students and the reader.
He uses traditional Japanese analogies like the bell and
its ability to make sound, examples from daily life, and
natural phenomena; he explains in detail Buddhist ter-
minology and formulae that are only briefly referred to

in the text, such as emptiness, thusness, karma, and the four erroneous views of phenomena. In the course of his commentary he makes us familiar with passages and ideas from other sutras and introduces us to many of the sayings and doings of Zen masters over the ages. Roshi's comments on Master Nyuri's questions and Emmon's responses help readers to find their own awakening and true nature in the ceasing of notions. In conclusion Roshi comments:

> "When even the last traces are gone" is when all the dirt of delusions has been washed off, together with the soap of the teaching, training, and enlightenment, and nothing at all remains— no smell of Zen, no ideology, no philosophy, no Buddha. Then the true nature functions freely and without any obstacles.

Martin Collcutt
Princeton University

NOTES

1. In Robert M. Gimello and Peter N. Gregory, eds., *Studies in Ch'an and Hua Yen* (Honolulu: University of Hawaii Press, 1983).
2. Ibid., 173.
3. *Dialog über das Auslöschen der Anschauung* (Frankfurt am Main: R. G. Fischer Verlag, 1987).
4. Gishin Tokiwa, trans., *A Dialogue on Contemplation Extinguished: Translated from the Chueh-kuan lun, an Early Chinese Zen Text from Tun Huang* (Kyoto: Institute for Zen Studies, 1973).

5. Sekida, Katsuki, trans., *Two Zen Classics: Mumonkan and Heki-ganroku* (New York: Weatherhill, 1977).
6. William M. Bodiford, *Soto Zen in Medieval Japan* (Honolulu: University of Hawaii Press, 1993).
7. Thomas Cleary, *Secrets of the Blue Cliff Record: Comments by Hakuin and Tenkei* (Boston: Shambhala Publications, 2000).

A Treatise on the Ceasing of Notions

AN INSTRUCTIVE TALK BETWEEN
MASTER NYURI AND DISCIPLE EMMON

*Emmon asks the questions,
and Master Nyuri's answers are given
in order to resolve his doubts.*

I

1a The Great Way is without limit, fathomless and subtle, beyond comprehension, beyond words.

Master Nyuri (whose name means "Entrance into the Principle") and his disciple Emmon ("Gate of Affinities") are discussing the truth.

THUS AT THE VERY OUTSET two statements are made about the Way that may be difficult to understand. It is said that the way is "fathomless and subtle." What does that mean? In order to clarify this, the Japanese term *innen* needs to be explained. *In* means the direct inner cause, the reason why; *en* are the conditions of *in*.

This may seem abstruse, but it can be illustrated by the analogy of a bell. Its ability to make or emit a sound is *in*; what brings forth the sound, the clapper for example, is *en*. Only when bell and clapper, *in* and *en*, come together, do they give rise to sound; that is, a phenomenon comes to be, appears, or manifests. In this way all phenomena, without exception, come to be and cease to be. All are dependent on *in* and *en* for their formation, hence they are without a separate self.

Now, all *in* and all *en* exist in the Great Way, not as discrete, independent, continuous entities, but fathomless and subtle, constantly changing.

The two persons who are talking about the Way are Master Nyuri and his disciple Emmon. The name Nyuri is composed of two Chinese characters: *nyu* means going in, entering, or coming in, and *ri* is truth, principle, reason, or the fitness of things. Thus Master Nyuri is one who has entered truth, has awakened.

The disciple's name, Emmon, also consists of two characters and is made up of *em*, which means affinity or connection, and *mon*, which is the character for gate. So Emmon is the one who in his search for enlightenment has arrived at the gate but has not yet entered.

⫸ **1b The Master was silent and said nothing.**

Emmon suddenly rose and asked, "What is called the heart? And how is the heart pacified?"

The Master answered, "You should not assume a heart, then there is no need to pacify it. That is called pacifying the heart."

Bodhidharma (circa 470–543) is the twenty-eighth Indian patriarch in the line after Sakyamuni Buddha, and the first Chinese Zen patriarch. In the transmission of Zen Buddhism, the Dharma is handed on to disciples whose realization is of a depth equal to that of the master. Hence, Bodhidharma's primary goal would have been finding one disciple able to receive the transmission of the Dharma, rather than spreading and popularizing Buddhism.

When Bodhidharma arrived in China from India, he found that Buddhism there was considered a subject for scholars only and that it was moreover extremely formal and ceremonious. In contrast, his way of teaching was unusual and fresh. This line or school, which began with Bodhidharma, is called the Dharma School, the Buddha Heart School, or the Zen School. It is best illustrated by the account of his meeting with the monk Taiso Eka (in Chinese, Dazu Huike, 487–593).

Though Eka was a scholar of both Confucianism and Buddhism, his heart was not really at peace and he was restless and worried. So he went to see Bodhidharma who was residing nearby and asked for his teaching. But Bodhidharma was sitting in meditation and did not even turn round. This continued for some time. Then on the eighth of December it began to snow. By the next morning Eka, who had been standing at the gate throughout the night, was knee-deep in snow. Bodhidharma, seeing him thus, addressed him for the first time. Eka, with tears in his eyes, said, "Please show compassion for me and teach me the Dharma that opens the gate of peace." Bodhidharma responded, "For long eons, all the buddhas have for the sake of the Dharma endured what cannot be endured, completed what cannot be completed. How can you, of fickle heart and small purpose, of shallow insight and little virtue, expect to see the truth? Training with a conceited and lazy heart is indeed laboring in vain."

Eka, as proof of his desperate determination, cut off his arm and presented it to Bodhidharma. (Do not mistake Eka's deed for gruesome self-torture! Hacking off his arm was his gesture of separating himself from all his past insufficient experiences and limited understanding; it was to empty himself to be ready to receive Bodhidharma's teaching.) He then asked Bodhidharma, "My heart is not at peace, please put my heart at rest." Bodhidharma countered, "Put your heart before me and I shall bring it to rest." At that, Eka tried to do so, but he had to admit, "My heart does not stop for one moment, it moves about freely and I cannot find nor get hold of it." "There, I have put your heart at rest for you," replied Bodhidharma, nodding. Eka, inheriting the transmission from Bodhidharma, became the second Chinese Zen patriarch.

The only way for truly putting the heart at rest is seeing into the nature of one's own heart. This seeing into its nature, *kensho* in Japanese, is the sole purpose of Zen. In *A Treatise on the Ceasing of Notions*, too, the first question is on the problem of putting the heart to rest. Bodhidharma merely pointed out to Eka what he should look for, and Eka obeyed. He did not waste his time with idle questions about the heart, but saw immediately. Zen training is just such a direct pointing, and consequently later generations in China called it a "direct pointing at the human heart, seeing into its nature, and becoming Buddha." The pointing is done by the teacher, but the seeing is entirely the affair of the disciple. Emmon, how-

ever, tries for a long while to grasp the heart by means
of Nyuri's explanations without trying to see himself.
So he puts question after question and keeps on asking.
And yet from the first question it is already obvious that
he is somehow trying to fit the heart into this world of
discrimination and phenomena; the absolute, however,
does not allow itself to be arranged into any system. What
Emmon wants is to define and pin the heart down, hence
the "peace" he aims for is in fact stopping and blocking
the heart. Master Nyuri answers him with kindness and
patience. The free activity of the heart is peace.

**≫2 Emmon: "But if there is no heart, then how can we learn
the Way?"**

**Nyuri: "The heart cannot conceive of the Way; so why
should the Way depend on the heart?"**

For an understanding of the text, and especially so for
Master Nyuri's answers, it is important to recognize the
misconceptions and delusions out of which Emmon's
questions arise. It will often seem as though Master
Nyuri's answers do not respond to Emmon's questions.
But Master Nyuri seizes Emmon's delusions right at the
root. His answers are prompted from there. Emmon's
second question shows us that he already differentiates
between heart and the Way. Master Nyuri's response
informs Emmon that the Way and the heart are not two
separate things.

3 Emmon: "If the Way cannot be conceived of by the heart, how can it be conceived or thought of?"

Nyuri: "As soon as a thought arises, there is also heart. Heart is contrary to the Way. No-thought is no-heart. No-heart is the Way of the Truth, or True Awakening."

Having a notion means that the heart is blocked and bound. And having no notions or thoughts is no-heart or empty heart (in Japanese, *mushin*): free, unrestricted functioning of the heart. No-heart, this free activity of the heart, is already the Way, and the Way is the truth.

4 Emmon: "Do all sentient beings have this heart or not?"

Nyuri: "That all sentient beings really have this heart is a mistaken view. To set up a heart within no-heart, in empty heart, only serves to create erroneous ideas."

It is obvious that one of Emmon's deep-rooted delusions is the notion of a heart as a constant, permanent, and unchanging entity. This is one of the four erroneous views of phenomena, or *shitendo* in Japanese:

1 The view that what is in constant change is lasting and permanent. This means to not realize that all phenomena are subject to constant change and rather to hold them as lasting and permanent.

2 The view that suffering is happiness. This is to assume one's own notions to be self-evident and to understand happiness as the fulfillment of these. This, however, means not realizing that reality—our life

from birth through sickness and old age to death—does not obey our own wishes and is not subject to our control, but rather is the activity of a power that is beyond all possible conceptions.

3 To take as "I" or "self" what in fact is No-I or no-self. This means not to see that all forms are devoid of a permanent, unchanging self and rather to assume an inherent and everlasting self in all forms.

4 To see as pure what is impure, to set up arbitrary distinctions between beautiful and ugly, and not to realize that what is called beautiful now (for instance a beautiful woman) with time changes into what is called ugly. This is actually two mistakes: the first is to differentiate what is beautiful and what is ugly; the second, consequent on the first, is to then become tied to beauty and thus be unaware of the ugly, which is already the other face of beauty. This results in clinging to beauty and ignoring or refusing the ugly.

≥ 5 Emmon: "What exists within no-heart?"

Nyuri: "No-heart equals no-thing. No-thing equals True Nature itself. And True Nature is the Great Way."

≥ 6 Emmon: "How can delusions of sentient beings be eradicated?"

Nyuri: "As long as one sees delusions and their eradication, one cannot shed them."

Originally there are no delusions. But if we arbitrarily assume them, that is take for real something that does not exist—and then want to eradicate it—that is delusion.

⫸7 Emmon: "Is it possible to be at one with the Way without having eradicated the delusions?"

Nyuri: "As long as one thinks of being at one with and not being at one with, one is not free of delusions."

Emmon asks whether it is possible to be at one with the Way while still harboring delusions—that is, he still takes the existence of delusions for granted.

⫸8 Emmon: "What should one do then?"

Nyuri: "Not doing anything—that's it!"

Not-doing does not mean doing nothing but rather means doing without the dualistic split into subject and object—that is, without a self that does the doing. This is then the intentionless doing that naturally and of itself responds (accurately and fittingly) to the situation.

II

1 Emmon asks, "What does a buddha eradicate and what does he attain in order to be called a buddha?"

Master Nyuri answers, "Without having eradicated anything, without attaining anything, he already is Buddha."

EMMON HAS a whole array of standards with which he classifies and judges, such as profound and shallow, right and wrong, good and bad, etc. He now wants to know if these are correct.

Master Nyuri's response is that there is nothing in the absolute or in phenomena to be eradicated and nothing to be attained. Without any value judgments, everything is complete as it is. But Emmon, caught up in his preconceptions, does not understand. He still believes that ordinary men are unawakened because they lack a correct standard. A buddha, so Emmon believes, has the ultimate and correct standard. Master Nyuri's denial of this causes his next question.

2 Emmon: "If he neither eradicates anything nor attains anything, how then does he differ from an ordinary human being?"

Nyuri: "He is not like one, because ordinary human beings all erroneously believe they have something to eradicate and mistakenly think that they have something to attain."

The use of a standard causes things to get divided into what one wants to attain and what one wants to get rid of. Only by evaluation according to a standard are things judged as right and wrong. The difference between ordinary men and buddhas is not the correctness of their standards but that buddhas have no standards.

3 Emmon: "Now you are saying that ordinary beings have something to attain but that buddhas do not. What then is the difference between attaining and not-attaining?"

Nyuri: "Delusion arises because ordinary beings want to attain something. Buddhas are free from delusions because they do not wish to attain anything. Within delusion arises at once division into same and not same. Without delusion there is neither difference nor nondifference."

For Emmon, attaining or not-attaining is a problem, because he is caught up in the notion of a separate and individual self. This immediately establishes an inside and an outside, a self and what seems to be other than self. Thus deluded, there is then one who wants to attain and something that needs to be attained. He cannot realize that all appearances are but manifestations of the One Truth.

4 Emmon: "If there is no difference, why then coin the name 'buddha'?"

Nyuri: "'Ordinary men' and 'buddha' are both just names. As names they are the same, without difference. It is as if one were speaking about the hair of a tortoise or about the horns of a hare."

The Chinese proverb of the hairs of a tortoise and the horns of a hare is a metaphor for what is erroneously believed to exist but in reality does not.

5 Emmon: "If the Buddha is like the hairs of a tortoise or the horns of a hare, then it can be said that he does not exist at all. What are you trying to teach?"

Nyuri: "I say that there is no such thing as the hairs of a tortoise, but I do not state that there is no tortoise. Why do you reproach me?"

Be careful! You are now probably thinking that since there is nothing to be obtained from the outside, it must be got from the inside. But if you harbor such notions, the tortoise at once grows hairs again. Why? Because we do not train to attain something but in order to realize what has always been there.

≫6 Emmon: "What do you mean by saying there is no such thing as the hairs, and what then does the tortoise mean?"

Nyuri: "The tortoise is analogous to the Way, and the hairs point at the self. Buddha is without self and thus is the Way. Ordinary men are obsessed with names and the preconception of self—this is how they are different from the Buddha—and so are convinced that the tortoise has hairs and that the hare has horns."

To be obsessed with names and notions—that is, to cling to a permanent and unchangeable self—means to not see the truth and instead to be possessed by arbitrary notions about it.

≫7 Emmon: "If that is so, then one could say that there is the Way but there is no self. When one says that something is, or that something is not, is one then not back at the view of either existence or nonexistence?"

Nyuri: "There is neither an existence of the Way nor is there a nonexistence of a self. Why? The tortoise is not something that did not exist in the past but exists now in the present, and so it cannot be referred to as existing. The hairs are not something that did exist in the past but do not in the present, and so one cannot refer to them as nonexisting. The same analogy holds good for the Way and the self."

Emmon is taking up the preceding answer. By starting his query with "If that is so," he shows that he does not recognize the truth when he hears it. All his questions come from his own categories into which he has classified his individual notions of truth. So he assumes that Master Nyuri, too, expresses only his own views and conceptions of truth. Emmon's mistake is that he holds to a logic, assuming it to be correct. Using this logic as a standard for evaluating Master Nyuri's answers, he is already distorting them. But Nyuri's answers are not logical, they are true—originating from personal experience of the universal truth.

Together with the notion of an individual and unchanging self arises the view of coming to be and ceasing to be, of birth and death. However, the original life or principle that is inherent in everything is beyond coming to be and ceasing to be. It is therefore not something that did not exist before but is now, or that existed earlier but is now no longer. Accordingly, it is apart from (or other than) both being and nonbeing, existence or nonexistence.

≫ 8 Emmon: "As for the seekers of the Way, does one attain it or do many find it? Does each one individually attain it, or is its attainment common to all? Is it originally inherent in all human beings, or is it attained only by training?"

Nyuri: "All your assumptions are false. Why? If the Way were but the attainment of one person, it would not be universal. And if it were the attainment of many, it would become exhausted. Further, if its attainment were individual, it would be a question of numbers. And if it were common to all, there would be no use for practice. If all had it from the beginning, then the ten thousand practices would be futile. And if one could attain it after completion of the training, it would be artificial and would not be the truth."

If the Way were not universal, it would not be the truth. If it were individual to each—that is, if everyone were to find their own distinct Way—then there would be a number of different Ways! And if the Way were common to all—that is, if everyone, however deluded, could attain it—then to practice it would have no meaning. If everyone already from the beginning had the Way, as conceived by Emmon as a definite Way with inherent values, then even endless practice and effort would be to no avail. And if one were to attain the Way by training as Emmon understands it—that is, by a practice encompassing the opposites of subject and object, of who practices and that which is practiced—it would constitute an artificial Way, for it would be contrived, thus arising out of separation between self and nature, and so subject to value judgments.

▶9 Emmon: "What then is it?"

Nyuri: "Free of all standards, discriminations, and desires."

III

▶ 1 Emmon asks, "The ordinary person has a body; he sees, hears, feels, and knows. The Buddha also has a body and sees, hears, feels, and knows. How then do they differ?"

Master Nyuri answers, "The ordinary man sees with the eyes, hears with the ears, feels with the body, and knows with the heart. But this is not so with the Buddha. With him seeing is not seeing with the eyes and knowing is not knowing with the heart. Why? Because it is beyond all limitations."

THE INHERENT FACULTY to see, hear, feel, and know originates from the true nature. But the ordinary person lives under the delusion that he sees with the eyes and hears with the ears. Not realizing it is an impermanent manifestation of the true nature, he believes this limited physical body of his to be his true nature and that seeing, hearing, feeling, and knowing are the free functions of this nature.

▥2 Emmon: "Why then is it said in the scriptures that the Buddha neither sees, nor hears, nor feels, nor knows?"

Nyuri: "The seeing, hearing, feeling, and knowing of a buddha is not that of the common man. But that does not mean that for him the world of perceptions does not exist; it only means that it is not limited by pairs of opposites such as being and not being, having and not having—and so is beyond all value judgments."

The Enlightened One is not caught up in the view of a continuous self, nor in the view of nothing. He is neither attached nor deluded. He manifests the true nature that, though changing from moment to moment, is yet fully present and absolute in each moment.

▥3 Emmon: "Does the objective world that the common man perceives have a real existence?"

Nyuri: "Not in reality, but it exists in delusion. Originally all is calm and quiet, but if mistakenly things are picked up and clung to, it at once turns into delusory existence."

An ordinary person exists as if in a dream. However, what he experiences while dreaming vanishes as soon as he awakens because the dream state is not real. Just as in a dream, one may plummet down endlessly into an abyss while actually lying safely in bed, so only on waking does one realize that one was always safe and never far away. Thus what seemed so real and concrete in the dream did not exist in reality.

>> 4 Emmon: "I cannot understand that. Why is the seeing of the Buddha not seeing with the eyes and his knowing not knowing with the mind?"

Nyuri: "It is extremely difficult to see into the self-nature of the Dharma. An analogy may help. When the subtle black light reflects things, it seems as if both that which reflects and that which is reflected really exist. Just as the eye that sees cannot see itself, and also as yin and yang act on things, it seems as if both that which knows and that which is known exist separately. But there is no mind that can know—no thing that can do the knowing—hence the mind that knows cannot know itself."

The term "black light" is used to indicate the light of truth, the buddha wisdom. It is the light that reflects all things in their suchness, as they are. Neither discriminating nor judging, it sees everything as equal and the same, and as that it is the wisdom of wonderful awareness, free of all the delusions of an individual, unchanging self.

With reference to the unity of that which is known and that which knows, of object and subject, the Platform Sutra of Eno (in Chinese, Huineng; 638–713), says that meditation and wisdom are "like a lamp and its light. If there is a lamp, there is also light. If the lamp is the body of the light, the light is the function of the lamp. Though these are two names, they are, in reality, the same."

IV

≫| Emmon rises and asks, "Then what does the Way ulti-
mately depend on?"

Master Nyuri answers, "Ultimately it does not depend
on anything; like emptiness, it relies on nothing. If the
Way did depend on anything there would be stopping
and starting, lord and retainer."

E MMON'S QUESTION arises from his conviction that
a creator and the created exist separately. He still
divides into subject and object. Our deep-rooted and
ingrained habit is to make pictures, graven images, so as
to render perceptible and set up what is imperceptible
and ineffable. In order to root out and eradicate this
habit, Zen Buddhism uses the concept of emptiness, or
sunyata in Sanskrit. Thus emptiness is a name for something that cannot be designated because it does not exist
relative to other things. Emptiness means that which has
no permanent form and can thus manifest in any form.
Or it could also be said that a thing is emptiness that has
become form. Just that is the gist of the Heart Sutra:
"Form is emptiness, emptiness is form."

》2 Emmon: "Then where does the Way itself come from and what is the functioning of the Dharma?"

Nyuri: "The Way comes from emptiness, and all things are the functioning of the Dharma."

》3 Emmon: "And who makes it function?"

Nyuri: "Nobody makes it function—the Dharma-realm functions of itself, according to its own nature."

Emmon assumes a creative agency, a doer.

》4 Emmon: "Is the Dharma-realm not subject to the power of the karma of sentient beings?"

Nyuri: "Whoever is karmically motivated is subject to karma and can no longer function freely. How could one who is not free to function dig the ocean, pile up mountains, set heaven at ease, and create the earth?"

Now Emmon has in mind a subject patiently enduring the decrees of fate. But neither the notion of an active nor passive subject is correct. There is no individual object that is acted on by a predestined karma, nor is there an individual subject that causes activity, for both these notions erroneously posit a fixed and predetermined fate or destiny.

That karma exists is beyond doubt. One who is not bound by karma is one who perceives the unity of cause and effect. The action of No-I smoothly responds to the given situation, without thinking of gain or loss, good or bad, without wanting to cause specific results; this is also called the "samadhi of cause and effect."

≫5   Emmon: "As I have heard, a bodhisattva can create his body by mental power. Does that not mean he uses supernormal powers?"

Nyuri: "The ordinary person's deeds are activated by karmic outflows, but the Buddha's actions are without leaks. Though there is a difference between them, neither case is the freely functioning Way. It is said in a sutra, 'As to the various bodies produced by the power of thought, all are but mental formations.'"

Karmic outflows (in Sanskrit, *asrava*) from the actions of ordinary men manifest as their passions, wants, sufferings, and sorrows. They arise because the true nature has been lost sight of. But however free of these one may have become, if one now leans on one's understanding, one has only replaced delusion with enlightenment—and that is not the Way. One genuinely enlightened is free of both delusion and enlightenment.

≫6   Emmon: "Earlier on you said that the Way comes from emptiness. Is emptiness then the same as Buddha?"

Nyuri: "Yes, the same."

Emmon produces yet another measuring stick with which to classify emptiness. He is incapable of thinking without such limitations.

Let me ask you, what is Buddha? To destroy the moment of delusion is enlightenment, but to hold on to the moment of enlightenment is once more delusion. And to define enlightenment as this or that is opinion.

≫7 Emmon: "But if he is emptiness, then why did the Buddha not guide people toward emptiness rather than teaching them to repeat his name?"

Nyuri: "Ordinary people are taught to repeat the name of the Buddha. The teachings of insight into the true form of the self are for those who know the Way. This is insight into the Buddha, for it is said that true form is no-form or emptiness."

Buddha-worship can help to eradicate the notion of a self as a distinct entity separate from the outside surroundings. Yet the Buddha who can be worshipped is but a conceptual buddha and needs to be gotten out of the way in order to be able to awaken to the true Buddha. Relevant to this is a dialogue between the Chinese Master Ummon Bunen (in Chinese, Yunmen Wenyan; 864–949) and a monk who asked him, "Having killed father and mother, one can go to the Buddha for repentance"—that is, clinging to one's body as one's possession and thus clinging to a permanent self, one can take refuge in the Buddha and thus create a new authority—"but having killed the Buddha and the patriarchs, where then could one turn for repentance?" Ummon answered, "It reveals itself."

And Master Rinzai Gigen (in Chinese, Linji Yixuan; died in 866), founder of the Rinzai School of Zen Buddhism, said, "When you meet the Buddha, kill the Buddha. When you meet the patriarchs, kill the patriarchs."

V

1 Emmon rises and asks, "I have heard that not only bodhisattvas but the followers of other Ways also attain the five supernormal powers. How do they differ?"

Master Nyuri answers, "They differ in that the followers of other Ways believe that there is someone who possesses something, whereas bodhisattvas do not think so. Why not? Because they have fully realized that there is no self."

THE FIVE SUPERNORMAL POWERS of the other Ways, or other religions, are:

1 To see what is invisible to others;
2 To hear what is inaudible to others;
3 To see into the future and to know the past;
4 To know others' thoughts;
5 To appear at will at any place.

But when a monk asked Master Rinzai what the supernormal powers and the Buddhist teachings on supernormal powers were, Rinzai answered:

1 In the realm of seeing not to be deceived by form;
2 In the realm of hearing not to be deceived by sound;
3 In the realm of smelling not to be deceived by odors;
4 In the realm of tasting not to be deceived by taste;
5 In the realm of thinking not to be deceived by notions.

That is the truly independent man.

These two versions clearly illustrate the difference between what followers of other Ways consider to be the supernormal powers and the Buddhist teachings on the powers of a bodhisattva. The former assume a self that attains and possesses these powers, whereas the latter posits a not-self (or true nature) that does not need to be attained and is not bound by any notion of attainment.

▥2 Emmon: "From of old, the beginner's realization of the Way is incomplete. Only dimly does he or she see the truth, and he or she understands only superficially the profound and subtle principle. What makes such a one superior to the followers of other Ways who have the five supernormal powers?"

Nyuri: "First of all, however hazily, grasp the principle yourself! Why make an issue out of the five supernormal powers of the other Ways?"

Emmon believes that someone is highly advanced if he or she has acquired much knowledge and learning. He has not yet realized the wondrously subtle functioning of the non-self and so is still caught up in the notion that training means the attainment of something that one did not have before.

Realization is not a gradual process but happens suddenly. A well-known saying expresses this: "In one leap directly becoming Buddha." In the Chinese translation of a now-lost Sanskrit sutra collection, enlightenment is described as "Where there is light, there is no darkness." Darkness does not fade away gradually while light gradually increases. Huineng, the sixth Patriarch, said, "The instant the Dharma-wisdom appears and blazes out, all false notions vanish at once." Or again, "Just as a lamp undoes the darkness of a thousand years, so one ray of wisdom expels ten thousand years of ignorance."

Realization as such is sudden, but the Way to it is fast or slow depending on the degree of delusion. Those who know that their own nature is one with the Way are fast. Those who look for the Way outside are bound to be slow. Hence Nyuri admonishes, "First of all, however hazily, grasp the principle yourself!"—thus employing skillful means to cut through Emmon's speculative views.

》3 Emmon: "One who has the five supernormal powers is highly esteemed by others, for he has preknowledge of future events, knows the past, and can guard himself against committing faults. Is this not a superior man?"

Nyuri: "No. Only worldlings are attached to form, are greedy to do business, are deceitful and confuse the truth. Even if one possessed the supernormal powers of the mendicant monk Shengyi, or the eloquence of Bhikkhu Shanxing, yet did not grasp the principle of true form, it is to be feared that he or she would share their misfortune, for the ground opened under their feet and they fell straight into hell."

According to the Shohomugyo Sutra (Sutra on the Inactivity of All Things), the mendicant monk Shengyi, or Shoi in Japanese, fell straight into hell. The Nirvana Sutra tells of the Bhikkhu Shanxing, or Zensho in Japanese, who possessed demonic eloquence and because of it the ground opened under his feet and he plummeted into the nethermost hell.

VI

≫1 Emmon asks, "Is the Way only in sentient beings or do grasses and trees also have it?"

Master Nyuri answers, "The Way pervades everything without exception."

E MMON'S GREAT ERROR is his view that enlightenment produces truth and that for this to take place a producer or creator is needed—a distinct and individual self. This, his view of a self, causes his question about sentient beings. Enlightenment, however, does not mean *to produce truth* but is rather the discovery of truth.

≫2 Emmon: "If the Way pervades everything, why then is killing against the precepts whereas the cutting of grasses or felling of trees is no offense?"

Nyuri: "To talk about offense and precepts is setting up subjective value judgments—hence, it is biased and not the true Way. Because ordinary worldlings have no understanding of the Way, they take a self for granted and so killing becomes conscious intention; consequently the heart gets bound and karma results, and one speaks of faults. But grasses and trees have no such bias and so are inherently at one with the Way, and since truth is without a self, who kills them is free of intentional murder. Hence arguments about offense or no offense are beside the point.

Those who are without a self, and so are at one with the Way, regard their bodies as they would regard grasses and trees. Even though pierced by a sword they are just like a tree in the woods. Therefore, when Manjushri raised his sword against Gautama Buddha, or when Angulimala lifted a dagger against Shakyamuni, that too is in accordance with the Way. Both perceived the principle of the unborn, the unoriginated, and realized that all phenomena are empty and void. As to that, there is no argument about offense or no offense."

Subjective value judgments are manmade and are concerned with moral standards. So the first part of the answer is an explanation in moral terms. The second part of the answer, however, beginning with "Those who are without a self, and so are at one with the Way" is an expression of the truth. Truth has its source in unending life as such, without birth and death, the Great Life. Individual forms or phenomena come and go; in their momentariness they reveal the Great Life, and thus each single one, while it lasts, is meaningful and precious.

▶3 Emmon: "If from the beginning trees and grasses are in accord with the Way, why do the sutras refer only to men and not also to trees and grasses?"

Nyuri: "But they do not refer to men only. The enlightenment of trees and grasses is also mentioned. One sutra says, 'The smallest speck of dust contains all the dharmas.' And again, 'All the dharmas are Thusness and all sentient beings are also Thusness. There are no two Thusnesses; nor are there any differences in Thusness.'"

Thusness, *tathata*, means everything just as it is, the nature of truth, "just so." Grasses, trees, men, all manifested forms reveal the truth or are the appearance of the truth. But men do not perceive truth as such, just as it is, and rather seek it elsewhere. Therefore, to become aware again that everything, just as it is, in its suchness, is the truth is called the attainment of buddhahood. This does not mean that bad men are converted to become good and then become Buddha. In the Bible, too, it is said, "Seek and you will find, knock and it will be opened unto you." Only if one seeks with all one's heart, and knocks with all one's might, is it possible to realize that the gate has always been open and that everything has always been just as it is. This realization is called enlightenment.

VII

1 Emmon asks, "As for the principle of ultimate emptiness, how can it be proven and verified?"

Master Nyuri answers, "Seek it in all forms, confirm it in your own words."

EMMON WOULD LIKE to have some proof of emptiness. But just as one can only know heat and cold if one has felt it oneself, so one can only know emptiness if one has experienced it oneself. This is then one's own proof or authentication.

2 Emmon: "How does one seek it in all forms and confirm it in one's own words?"

Nyuri: "Emptiness and forms are one. Words and confirmation are not two."

In Zen Buddhism, the nonduality of the true nature is expressed either by "not two," or *funi* in Japanese, or by "as one," *ichinyo* in Japanese.

▶3 Emmon: "If all existing things are empty, why can only buddhas see this and not ordinary people?"

Nyuri: "It is obscured by the working of error but becomes clear in the stillness of truth."

Value judgments give rise to arbitrary notions motivated by self-centeredness, and so they are contrary to the natural harmony.

▶4 Emmon: "If all forms are really empty, how can they get perfumed? Conversely, if they do get perfumed, how can they be empty? Or realize emptiness?"

Nyuri: "Speaking of what is false at once gives rise to the ordinary delusion and its workings. In true emptiness there is nothing that can attract perfumes."

Forms that arise from moment to moment out of the true nature and again sink back into it, into No-I, are without any individual self. Attempts to grasp the true nature in the form gives rise to the false assumption of a permanent and unchanging self. If, for instance, one asks what form water has, the usual reply is that water has no form. And yet, from moment to moment, water manifests itself in some form. Having seen water in a bowl and so believing it to be round in form would be the error caused by not being aware of the true nature. What has thus arisen by error becomes delusion; consequent on delusion, it has seeming existence. However, such a seemingly existing form can yet take on and does take on odor, can hurt, or may get dirty, whereas the true nature of emptiness does not.

▶5 Emmon: "If all forms are really empty, then surely there is no need to train in the Way. Is this because sentient beings are already by nature empty?"

Nyuri: "Once the principle of emptiness is realized, there is indeed no need for training. Delusions about existence arise only because emptiness has not been penetrated completely."

As a young monk, Master Dogen Kigen was plagued by the question of why, with true nature being inherently perfect and complete, it should be necessary to undergo any training. Since no one in Japan could answer that question for him, he traveled all the way to China to find out. After enlightenment he understood that "Even though one is originally Buddha, without training this cannot come into awareness for it does not reveal itself without enlightenment." This "letting Buddha reveal himself" is the full realization of emptiness.

▶6 Emmon: "In that case, to drop all delusions is to unite with the Way. Do you mean that all have gone astray?"

Nyuri: "By no means. Delusions are not the Way, but neither is letting go of delusions the Way. Why? For example, one who is drunk is not sober. And, if sober,

he is not drunk. Though the state of being drunk and being sober do not exist without each other, yet being drunk is not, at the same time, being sober."

There are those who are asleep and others who are awake, drunk ones and sober ones. But these states are all within the Way. Still caught up in ephemeral appearances, Emmon does not know the true nature, is not aware of the root and origin; consequently, he distinguishes between "apart from" and "at one with" the Way.

7 Emmon: "Where is the drunkenness after one has become sober?"

Nyuri: "It is like turning over the palm of one's hand. After having turned it over, why ask where it is?"

VIII

≫1 Emmon asks, "Can one who does not understand the principle preach the Dharma and instruct people?"

Master Nyuri answers, "Impossible! With his own eyes not yet clear, how can he make others see?"

BEFORE THE SIXTH PATRIARCH, Huineng, expounded the Platform Sutra, he entered into a state of deep enlightenment and remained silent for a long time. The Heart Sutra expresses the essence of all the Prajna Paramita teachings in only 272 Chinese characters, yet even thus concentrated it still begins when the Bodhisattva Kannon (or Avalokitesvara in Sanskrit) enters into deep meditation. This may seem incidental, yet the most important condition of all is to first find peace oneself and to become enlightened, before attempting to teach others.

≫2 Emmon: "But could he not use the power of his knowledge as a skillful means for teaching others?"

Nyuri: "In the case of someone who has realized the principle of the Way, one could call this the power of knowledge. But as to someone who has not yet realized the principle, it rather ought to be called the power of ignorance, for it merely furthers and encourages one's own afflicting passions."

⚫3 Emmon: "Though it may not be possible for him to instruct people about the principle of the Way, could he not, however, make them acquainted with the Ten Virtuous Deeds and the Five Precepts? Would he not help them thus and so enable them to be reborn into the human or heavenly realms?"

Nyuri: "From the point of the ultimate principle, not only is this of no benefit at all, but furthermore it invites two more mistakes—deceiving oneself and deceiving others. To deceive oneself means to obstruct oneself from attaining the Way. To deceive others means leaving them to stray about in the cycle of birth and death in the six realms."

The six realms are those of heavenly beings, fighting demigods, humans, animals, hungry ghosts, and the miserable realm of suffering hells. Emmon proceeds from the premise that these six realms exist and that it is propitious to be reborn in either the human or heavenly states. But since these six realms exist only within delusion, it is still possible to fall back into the miserable realm of suffering hells even from the heavenly realm. This latter, therefore, is not a true and permanent heaven, nor is its peace everlasting.

⧉ 4 Emmon: "Did not the Buddha expound different teachings for each of the five vehicles?"

Nyuri: "The Buddha did most certainly not teach different truths. Such impressions only arise from people's hopes and expectations and are but manifestations of them. Hence the Buddha says in a sutra, 'When the heart has become clean and empty, there is no vehicle, and no one who rides in it. This is the One Vehicle that I teach.'"

The five vehicles may also be seen as the various teachings intended to lead human beings into an ideal world. Thus the human vehicle is for being reborn into the human world; the heavenly vehicle facilitates rebirth in the heavenly state. Then there are respectively the vehicles of the *sravaka*, or hearers; of the *pratyekabuddhas*, or "solitary awakened ones"; and of the bodhisattvas. Of these five vehicles the first two are worldly, and the other three are supposed to lead from the world of delusion to the world of enlightenment.

IX

▶1 Emmon asks, "Why does a true man of the Way remain unknown; why is he not recognized by others?"

Master Nyuri answers, "Just as the pauper is unlikely to recognize a rare treasure, so the true man is beyond the understanding of the vulgar."

THE COMMON MAN does not see things in their suchness, as they really are, because of his arbitrary, biased judgments. By means of these he endeavors to separate and distinguish things so as to grasp them—and just because of this he is unable to see the truth.

▶2 Emmon: "There are many impostors who do not care for the true Dharma; they assume an air of dignity and chiefly spend their time occupying themselves with refined matters. Many men and women seek their company. Why is that?"

Nyuri: "Just as a loose woman attracts a lot of men, or as flies swarm around rotting meat, so reputation and name are powerful attractions."

$$X$$

1 Emmon asks, "How does a bodhisattva follow a round-about way and yet complete the Way of the Buddha?"

Master Nyuri answers, "He does not discriminate between good and bad."

E MMON'S QUESTION refers to the Vimalakirti Sutra, in which *agatim-gacchan*, or nontraditional, is used to refer to a roundabout path a bodhisattva might take for reasons of expediency, in order to reach all sentient beings.

Emmon believes there is a right way and a wrong one. But what he considers to be the right way is one-sided, limited, and hence within the realm of delusion. Only while deluded do we have notions of deviating from the Way. In truth not for a moment are we ever separated from the Way of the Buddha.

2 Emmon: "What is nondiscrimination?"

Nyuri: "The heart not giving rise to anything."

≫3 Emmon: "And as to the nondoer?"

Nyuri: "A nondoer is neither denied nor asserted."

There is no such thing as an unchanging, permanent form. But there is that which has no definite form and which is constantly changing. To put it succinctly, there is change but nothing permanent.

≫4 Emmon: "Is it then known without knowing?"

Nyuri: "Though knowing, there is no I who knows."

Though there is awareness of things, it is not bound by things.

≫5 Emmon: "If not I, who then knows?"

Nyuri: "Knowing is without an I."

≫6 Emmon: "What is the obstruction when speaking of I?"

Nyuri: "There is no obstruction in just using the name but I fear that the heart will get involved all too soon."

≫7 Emmon: "What is the obstruction if the heart gets involved?"

Nyuri: "Nonengagement equals nonobstruction. For if there is no engagement, what obstruction could there be?"

If not caught and tied up by anything, the heart is empty. And when the heart is empty, questions such as Emmon's could not arise.

⫸ 8 Emmon: "If you eschew the phenomenal and hold to nothing, how can you speak of roundabout paths?"

Nyuri: "In truth there is nothing. You try hard to posit something. What for?"

A bodhisattva refuses nothing and shows no preferences. Without pondering or judging whether Way or roundabout path, he acts in accordance with what the situation demands because he knows that the Way and the roundabout path are one.

⫸ 9 Emmon: "But if so, if there is affinity toward killing, might this not lead to the grave offense of killing?"

Nyuri: "A brush fire rages up the mountain slope, a gale uproots trees, a landslide buries animals, flood water drowns insects. If the heart is like this, killing a person is also possible. But when the heart is confused and sees life and death, then a single ant can hold your life in bondage."

If the heart goes astray—that is, if it gets caught up in picking and choosing—it differentiates between life and death. So it perceives this as good and that as bad but does not know of the true life of the unborn. In that state of unawareness, the killing of a single ant may result in tragedy.

▣ 10 Emmon: "And as to affinity for stealing?"

Nyuri: "Bees drink from flowers by the pond; sparrows peck millet in the farmyard; cows feed on the beans in the wetlands; horses graze on the grain in the fields. After all, if another's possession is not discriminated as such, even the summit of a mountain can be taken respectfully. Were this not so, a leaf as thin as needle-point could make a rope round your neck and enslave you."

Stealing does not begin at the moment one takes something, but as soon as one differentiates between oneself and others.

▣ 11 Emmon: "Are there also affinities that tend to sexual indulgence?"

Nyuri: "The sky vaults over the earth; yang and yin unite; piss flows into the latrine; spring water flows into the aqueduct. A heart like this is not obstructed by anything. But if selection brings about discrimination, then even one's own wife makes one feel lecherous."

▣ 12 Emmon: "And as to the affinities that can bring about lying?"

Nyuri: "Speaking, but there is no one who speaks; words uttered, yet they come from an empty heart. A voice like the sound of a bell, a breath like the sighing of the wind. If the heart is like this, then even what is named Buddha ceases. But if the heart is not like this, then even invoking the name of the Buddha is but a lie."

Delusion splits into two: subject and object, self and other, inside and outside. To recognize this as delusion and become aware of the unity of all things—seeing the Buddha in all things—is called the heart of kindness and compassion. Whatever words arise from such an insight are all true—whereas words that do not issue from it are lies.

≫1 Emmon rises and asks, "If the body is viewed as nonex-
istent, then what about walking, standing, sitting, and
lying down?"

Master Nyuri answers, "Just walk, stand, sit, lie down!
Why set up any views with regard to the body?"

EMMON STILL has not realized that there is no
doer.

≫2 Emmon: "Without keeping to the view of nonexistence, how can the right principle be pondered and
maintained?"

Nyuri: "If one holds that the heart exists, it exists even
though one does not think of anything. If the empty
heart is realized, the heart remains empty even while
thinking. How so? It is like a Zen master who sits undisturbed and quiet though thoughts arise or like the
heart that remains undisturbed and empty amid a rag-
ing gale."

While the previous question was concerned with physical activity, the issue now is spiritual functioning. For Emmon, caught up in the notion of a self as separate from others, there also exists the separation into part and whole, man and surrounding circumstances, subject and object. Based on that notion, Emmon reasons that the part must have a self and be able to control the whole. For him, the concept of doing wholeheartedly, or "the samadhi of doing," is confusing and is further fraught with the danger of no longer knowing what is good and bad.

Contrary to that, Master Nyuri's answer has its origin in the awareness of truth in which there is no separation whatever. The harmony of the natural order itself exercises a control, which is really no control, because there is neither a controller nor something to be controlled. There, the part and the whole are already "as one" or "not two."

XII

> I Emmon asks, "If an inexperienced beginner on the Way should suddenly encounter someone intent on killing him, what must he do to conform with the Way?"
>
> Master Nyuri answers, "Nothing special needs to be done, because if he can escape, he will do so. If he cannot escape, he will have to endure it. If it is endurable, he will have to suffer it out. If it is not endurable, he will cry out."

Emmon does not know the Great Life that, though wounded, is not itself wounded; though in the midst of dirt, does not get dirty; and does not get extinguished in death. For him, living correctly in accordance with the Way should therefore result in one's going through life unharmed and free from calamities. Hence he conceives of a buddha as someone no longer in danger of being killed; within Emmon's concepts, violent death is not in accord with the Way. As Emmon sees it, there are thus but two answers possible: either there is a perfect way to react to the situation, or there is a perfect way to escape. But such thinking in extremes is one of the three great errors—the other two being perverted or upside-down notions, and fanciful imaginings.

Master Nyuri's answer is that a response will arise quite naturally of itself from the Great Life. It needs no planning. And in this sense both being killed and surviving are in harmony with the Way. But for somebody whose actions are governed by his self-chosen values and judgments, consequent only upon his own shallow understanding and narrow experience, neither being killed nor surviving are in accord with the Way.

≫ 2 Emmon: "If he cries out, how then does he differ from one who still holds the view of I?"

Nyuri: "When a bell is struck with a mallet, the sound quite naturally comes out of itself. So why should one call it an I? But if, on being killed, you lay hold of the heart and constrain it, and endure silently with clenched teeth, this is sure to produce a superego!"

Emmon believes that an enlightened one is no longer moved by feelings of joy and sorrow, of like and dislike. He is not aware of the great and decisive difference between being moved by feelings and being stuck in attachments. To be moved by feelings is the free and unhindered flow of the heart in response to the things encountered, changing in response to things as they move. But attachment is the heart clinging to things or feelings and thus tying itself up. Still another cause for Emmon's error is that he fails to consider time. The precondition for correctly seeing what changes from moment to moment is not to remain static oneself but to harmoniously go with the change and so let the true function of the heart act freely. Then both laughing and crying are natural responses to circumstances. A problem only arises when there is a hesitation at this or that and thus the reaction is continued though the circumstance that produced it no longer continues.

Once again Emmon here mistakes form for the absolute and does not recognize that the immobility of the absolute is the capacity for movement in forms. For more of this discussion, see the analogy of mirror and film in the comment to section XV, dialogue 6.

▨3 Emmon: "A man who cries out in pain or grief is surely swayed by his feelings; how can that be the same as the sound from the bell?"

Nyuri: "Talking about same and not same only shows how confused you are. Your question arises from your own fancies and speculations. For if the heart is empty and makes no distinctions, the Way functions according to its own nature."

▨4 Emmon: "I have heard it said that the Buddha cannot be wounded by weapons, is not oppressed by suffering, cannot be compelled by forms, and that his heart does not get agitated. What does this mean?"

Nyuri: "If one fully realizes that all things are devoid of a self, then whether emitting a sound or not emitting a sound, whether agitated or not agitated, all accords with the principle of the Way, without let or hindrance."

Emmon believes that the physical body of a buddha cannot be wounded and that a buddha cannot feel grief or pain. But it is the buddha nature, not the physical body, that cannot be wounded though blood spurts high. Once a monk came to Joshu Jushin (in Chinese, Zhaozhou Congshen; 778–897), who was one of the greatest Chinese Zen masters. The monk asked Joshu what was the hardest thing in the world. Joshu answered, "If you wish to slander me, do not restrain yourself. If your own mouth is insufficient, take on the beak of a bird. And if you really want to insult me, just spit at me as much as you like. Should your own spittle be insufficient, take a bucket of water and pour it over me."

The above question and answer may not seem apposite, but what Joshu wants to demonstrate is this: that which is harder than any diamond is actually inherent in all of us. And that can neither be insulted nor dirtied, neither wounded nor shaken.

XIII ⬛

⬛⎮ Emmon asks, "I have seen followers of the Way who
are not fully dedicated; they do not carefully observe
the precepts; their demeanor is not always correct and
polite, nor is their behavior always dignified; and they
do not always help sentient beings. They seem to just
aimlessly waste their time. Why is this so?"

Master Nyuri answers, "Because they want to forget
all discriminations that arise in the heart and want
to destroy all the various views they have. So though
from the outside it may look as if they are aimless, yet
inwardly they are assiduously training and cultivating
themselves."

EMMON HAS IN MIND ways of training in which the
keeping of precepts and observance of the rules have
become of paramount importance. That makes for a very
formal training that sharply distinguishes between monk
and layman, good and bad, Way and not-Way. However,
a truly dedicated practitioner does not exclusively go
only by the rules. Rather, he lives naturally in accordance with the functioning of the No-I. What may seem

aimless is, in fact, the change taking place from moment to moment in response to prevailing (yet changing) circumstances and situations.

≫2   Emmon: "But if a practitioner holds such childish opinions, how can he destroy false views?"

Nyuri: "You had better destroy your own opinions! Why do you get worked up about those others? Why should a fish that escapes into the depths care whether the angler hates him?"

≫3   Emmon: "But if such a one, though he benefits himself, does bring harm to others, how can he be called a follower of the Great Vehicle?"

Nyuri: "If you do not produce such views, neither will the other. It is you who are now overly concerned with another's views—but these views have arisen in yourself, not in the other!"

In this question, Emmon differentiates between seeking enlightenment for oneself (*jiri*, in Japanese) and seeking enlightenment in order to help others (*rita*). He is not aware that these two are not different. In order to help others, one's own realization is the first condition, the essential insight into one's nature, and this at the same time also constitutes the realization of the supposed other.

A further misconception of Emmon's is that he believes

people have to be liberated. But in absolute truth, all sentient beings are already Buddha and so do not need to be liberated, only to be awakened from their dreams and delusions. Hence a master does not really lead a disciple to enlightenment but rather increases his sufferings that arise from delusion so that he may awaken from it. With his notion of liberation, Emmon merely piles one more delusion on top of his already existing ones.

≥4 Emmon: "One who inwardly is well versed in the principles of the Great Vehicle, yet presents outwardly the appearance of the Small Vehicle, can such a one harm the Dharma?"

Nyuri: "You are trying to force an old man to play the fool and indulge in childish games. Of what use is this to the principle?"

≥5 Emmon: "Who can recognize and know a bodhisattva who has destroyed all his notions?"

Nyuri: "Only one attained to the true Dharma can recognize him, only one trained can know him."

≥6 Emmon: "Can such a man of the Great Vehicle also help others to awake?"

Nyuri: "How could it be possible for sun and moon not to shine, or a lamp, when lifted high, not to cast its light all round?"

▶ 7 Emmon: "What skillful means will he employ?"

Nyuri: "Spontaneously right, without any skillful means."

Emmon is desperately looking for some technique he can cling to. He still cannot understand that instead he should let go of all techniques and hand himself over to the natural functioning of No-I.

▶ 8 Emmon: "But if he does not use any skillful means, how can he be of benefit to others?"

Nyuri: "Something emerges and is named; a matter arises and is responded to. The empty heart neither calculates nor compares, and so there is no occasion to plan ahead."

▶ 9 Emmon: "I hear that the Tathagata spent seven days in meditation before he devised his skillful means. So how can it be asserted that there is no deliberation or planning in the heart?"

Nyuri: "As for the state of the Buddha, it cannot be grasped by thought, cannot be approached by understanding, cannot be measured or learned."

Emmon still has the notion of a self. Accordingly his reflections are already mixed with convictions, notions, and expectations, all of which act as a screen to his seeing. But the pondering of a buddha is the functioning of

No-I: unalloyed and pure like a clear mirror that directly reflects everything in its suchness, just as it is.

The state of No-I or empty heart does not mean that thought is inhibited, nor does it mean being unaware of and unreceptive to what is. On the contrary, it means the natural reaction in response to all that appears without any selective value judgments. But it is beyond Emmon to realize that it is impossible for an I to understand No-I.

≫10 Emmon: "But how can Buddha lie?"

   Nyuri: "He speaks the truth; he does not deceive."

Though the Buddha says he has no deliberation in the heart, yet the sutras assert that the Buddha devised skillful means. So Emmon cannot but assume this to be a lie.

≫11 Emmon: "Why do the sutras then state that he pondered for seven days before setting up skillful means, if now you state that he did not?"

   Nyuri: "The skillful means were set up for teaching purposes."

Master Nyuri ignores Emmon's undiscerning question and clearly affirms once again that the object of the Buddha's pondering was for the guidance of others.

≫ 12 Emmon: "From where do all the buddhas and their skillful means come?"

Nyuri: "The buddhas are unoriginated, unborn; they are
creations of the heart. Though there are skillful means
for assisting all beings, the Dharma is fundamentally
without a name."

Master Nyuri is not concerned with forms, only with the
Great Life itself. This Great Life neither comes to be nor
ceases to be; it is beyond our understanding, ineffable.
It manifests dependent on and in response to causes
and conditions, to *innen*, but is itself without name and
form—indeed, without any characteristics at all.

XIV

1 Emmon asks, "I do not understand. What is called Buddha? What is called the Way? What is called change? What is called permanence?"

Master Nyuri answers, "Fully enlightened without anything further to do, that is called Buddha. Well-versed and full of insight into everything, that is called the Way. Transformation is the Dharma-realm manifesting as the changing forms. Final calm and extinction is the permanent."

2 Emmon: "What does it mean that all things are the Buddhadharma?"

Nyuri: "Whether things or not things, all are the Buddhadharma."

3 Emmon: "What is called 'thing,' what 'no-thing,' and what 'neither thing nor no-thing'?"

Nyuri: "What 'is' is called 'thing,' what 'is not' is called 'no-thing'; and what is not encompassed by either 'is' or 'is not' is called 'neither thing nor no-thing.'"

EMMON SEEKS to grasp the truth by means of Master Nyuri's words. Though he himself states that all things are the Buddhadharma, he does not try to see it himself. He attempts to grasp truth by means of words, rather than through direct and immediate perception of it.

The Confucian scholar Zhou Dunyi (or Shu Toni in Japanese), wanting to gain insight, went to train with Zen Master Huanglong Huinan (in Japanese, Oryo Enan; 1002–1069). Master Huinan told him, "You are a Confucian scholar. In the writings of Master Confucius, it is said, 'If one awakens to the truth in the morning, one can die happily at noon.' Do you know this precious truth?" In spite of all his learning, Zhou Dunyi was lost for an answer. So he went to another Zen master, Jinshan Foyin (in Japanese, Kinsan Butsuin; 1032–1098), and asked what this ultimate truth was. Foyin replied, "You see those blue mountains over there; nobody prevents your seeing." Zhou Dunyi did not quite understand and hesitated. Foyin burst out laughing. At that Zhou Dunyi attained insight.

⧗ 4 Emmon: "Who verifies this statement?"

Nyuri: "This statement is without who; why should you ask for it to be verified?"

Truth is present, always and everywhere, and is distinct and clear. It needs no proof or verification. Nor is this truth a creation of the Buddha or of any enlightened ones; as such, it is the truth itself.

≫5 Emmon: "If there is no one, who then states what?"

Nyuri: "No who, no statement—that is the true statement."

≫6 Emmon: "What, then, would be called a false statement?"

Nyuri: "The notion that there is something to state."

Emmon thinks it possible to grasp and possess the unchanging, eternal words of truth. He believes the experience of enlightenment to be something that, once received, is from that moment on one's inalienable property. But such thinking only indicates one's being caught in notions of words and experiences. What truly can be called enlightenment is, however, not to be caught in any truth, any words, any experience. Zen texts, therefore, continuously stress the necessity of washing away even the mere odor of enlightenment together with the dirt of training.

≫7 Emmon: "If this is being caught in thought, what then is no-thought?"

Nyuri: "Thought is but a word. Since words themselves are without any substance, thought, too, is empty."

In common with all other manifestations, words exist in dependence on causes and conditions. And since these causes and conditions undergo perpetual change, words, too, are subject to constant change. So they are void of any continuous entity—what remains of them is like the light of a star that has died long ago.

⊨8 Emmon: "If this accords with the teachings, then all sentient beings are from the beginning already enlightened tathagatas."

Nyuri: "Since there are no bonds, how can there be liberated beings?"

Doshin (in Chinese, Daoxin; 580–651), the fourth Chinese Zen patriarch, came to the third patriarch, Sosan (in Chinese, Sengcan; died 606), and asked to be liberated. Sosan responded, "Who put you under restraint?" Doshin replied, "No one." Sosan asked, "Then why are you seeking to be liberated?" At that, Doshin had great *satori*. As the story illustrates, there are no bonds to be freed from, nothing is lacking, and there is nothing that has to be gained by training. As was said in the very first sentence of this text, "The Great Way is without limit, fathomless and subtle."

9 Emmon: "What is the name of this Dharma?"

Nyuri: "There is no Dharma—even less a name."

10 Emmon: "If this is the teaching, I fail to understand it."

Nyuri: "Truly there is no teaching to be understood. Do not seek for understanding."

Emmon wants to make understanding into an object, into something that he can hold on to and that will not change. This clinging to something and thus tying oneself up is an ingrained habit of each of us.

11 Emmon: "And in the end, what?"

Nyuri: "No beginning and no end."

12 Emmon: "Then is there no cause and effect either?"

Nyuri: "Without beginning, there is no end."

Though Emmon is constantly looking for something that is permanent, all his questions refer to impermanent things or matters. Thus he even interprets Master Nyuri's answers as relating to conditioned forms; he fits them into his scheme of classification, when in fact these answers are given from the standpoint of the absolute. This is not done to make a fool of Emmon but in order to render truth perceptible, and to show that what we separate by means of words is in reality one.

≫13 Emmon: "How can this teaching then be verified?"

Nyuri: "Truth is not something that needs to be verified."

There is no other way than one's own experience. Truth cannot be taught or imparted by way of proof.

≫14 Emmon: "And how is it to be known and seen?"

Nyuri: "By knowing the suchness of all things—by seeing the equality of all things."

≫15 Emmon: "What heart knows? What eye sees?"

Nyuri: "The knowing of not-knowing, the seeing of not-seeing."

≫16 Emmon: "Who makes this statement?"

Nyuri: "This is what I ask myself, too."

≫17 Emmon: "What do you mean by, 'That is what I ask myself, too?'"

Nyuri: "If you ponder your own question, the answer will arise of itself."

Invariably the answer is already contained in the question.

18 At this, Emmon fell silent and pondered deeply. Master Nyuri then asked him, "Have you nothing more to say?"

Emmon answered, "I do not see one single thing, not even the tiniest speck of dust. There is nothing more to be said."

Thereupon Master Nyuri commented, "It seems that now you have glimpsed the principle of truth."

XV

1 Emmon asks, "Why do you say that I seem to have glimpsed rather than that I have correctly seen?"

Master Nyuri answers, "What you now have seen is the nonexistence of all things. That makes you like the followers of other Ways who study to become invisible, etc., and yet cannot lose their shadow nor hide their footprints."

EMMON HAS simply transposed his ideas of being and nonbeing. He still has not realized that being and nonbeing are one.

2 Emmon: "How can both form and shadow be eradicated?"

Nyuri: "In the origin there is neither heart nor object; do not give rise to opinions of things coming to be and ceasing to be."

3 Emmon: "The ordinary man asks questions; Buddha teaches, is that so?"

Nyuri: "Questions arise because of doubts; teaching is for the settling of doubts."

▶4 Emmon: "I have heard it said that the Buddha teaches even without being asked. What does he have to clarify? Is there a Dharma that has to be taught, or does his penetrating insight perceive the doubts of others?"

Nyuri: "It is all but the dispensing of medicine to cure specific ailments. Just as when thunder rolls in heaven, the echo answers."

▶5 Emmon: "Having no volitional intention to be born, why did the Great Holy Tathagata appear in the world?"

Nyuri: "In times of peace, sweet grass grows of itself."

Huang Tingjian (in Japanese, Ko Teiken) went to see Zen Master Huitang Zuxin (in Japanese, Maido Soshin; 1025–1100) for instruction. Huitang asked him, "Do you know the one saying of Confucius that completely accords with the spirit of Zen?" Huang Tingjian said that he did not know. Just at that time of year, the mignonettes were in full bloom and their scent pervaded the temple. Master Huitang asked, "Can you smell the mignonettes?" Huang Tingjian said, "Yes, very much so." "There, I am not hiding anything from you," stated Master Huitang.

Generally, a disciple believes that the master possesses the truth and that he dishes it out little by little. Therefore he always suspects that there is still something he has not been shown so far, a hidden or concealed truth. Emmon, too, has this idea. But factually, enlightened masters do not possess anything at all—and just because of this they see that all things, just as they are, are the manifestations of truth. One who has truly realized that, and knows that truth reveals itself always and everywhere, may be called "sweet grass."

≥6 Emmon: "Having no fixed lifespan that comes to an end, why then did the Tathagata reveal his nirvana and die?"

Nyuri: "In times of drought and famine, all crops perish."

Emmon's view of Buddha is as an unchanging being, not conditioned by anything and thus absolute. Therefore it seems contradictory to him that the Buddha who physically appeared should then also die again. He does not understand that it is the essence of what continuously changes that is unoriginated, unborn emptiness, that does not die.

For example, a mirror reflects everything just as it appears; consequently, the images thus reflected change constantly. What does not change is the mirror's faculty or nature to reflect. Contrary to that, the picture on a photographic film is static and unchangeable and it is the film itself that has changed by the exposure. Emmon's view of the absolute is analogous to that of the picture on a film. He does not realize that the body of the Buddha is like a reflection in a mirror, whereas impermanence itself is the real Buddha.

7 Emmon: "I have heard that because of the compassion in his heart the Buddha came out of samadhi, and out of pity helped many sentient beings toward awakening. How can such unobstructed great functioning be the same as sweet grass in favorable conditions?"

Nyuri: "Samadhi is called the dharmakaya, or Dharma body; the body made up of the four great elements is the sambhogakaya, or reward body; and what appears in response to circumstance is the nirmanakaya, or transformation body. The dharmakaya is not bound by anything; the transformation body is not subject to any karmic conditions but freely rises up and sinks again with nothing remaining—and so it is said to be unobstructed."

Buddha is the manifestation of truth. Grasses and trees, too, are the manifestation of truth. Emmon cannot understand this, and so for him Buddha and grasses are worlds apart. To make Emmon realize his delusion, Master Nyuri answers in terms of the three bodies of the Buddha: *dharmakaya*, *sambhogakaya*, and *nirmanakaya*. These three bodies are not three different entities but represent three aspects of truth: the essence or absolute, the form, and the function, respectively. That the transformation body is not subject to conditions means that it changes freely and of itself in response to the situation and that it leaves no traces. Not being fettered by conditions means changing with conditions.

≫8 Emmon: "What is called compassion?"

Nyuri: "The transformation body responds fully without thinking to the true voidness. Benevolence toward beings is free of any intention and springs from an empty heart. If forced to give it a name, it is called compassion."

≫9 Emmon: "When will sentient beings who attain the Way become like the Tathagata?"

Nyuri: "If they have not yet completed it, though they may practice the Way for as many eons as there are grains of sand in the Ganges, they are yet far, far from arriving. But once completed, the very sentient being has become the Tathagata. Why should you worry whether they can become Tathagata or not?"

Emmon commits the same error again and again. He thinks that training is the means to effect buddhahood! He still cannot conceive that it is the realization of the truth that has always been there and from which we have never been separated.

≫ 10 **Emmon: "If this is your teaching, then the state of a tathagata should be easy to attain. Why is it then said that it demands practicing for three great eons?"**

Nyuri: "It is indeed most difficult."

It is indeed the most difficult thing to realize that without doing anything one is already Buddha. However, without doing anything does not mean to let delusions persist just as they are, and to try to see Buddha in them. It rather means to realize truth without creating delusions and without eradicating them.

≫ 11 **Emmon: "If this very body, without any further cultivation, already is Tathagata, why do you call it most difficult?"**

Nyuri: "To arouse the heart is easy; to eradicate the heart is difficult indeed. To affirm the body, or oneself, is easy; to deny the body is difficult. It is easy to act, but difficult to refrain from doing anything. Know therefore that profound achievement is difficult to comprehend, and that it is hard indeed to come into union with the mysterious principle. The immovable is the truth. Even the three sages hardly match it."

Nothing factual is known of who these three sages are. Though there are innumerable speculations as to their identity, these seem dubious.

▓ 12 At this, Emmon sighed deeply. That sound filled the ten directions. Suddenly the sound stopped and he had great satori. The mysterious light of clear wisdom radiated of itself and dispelled all doubt. Only now he knew how hard it is to follow the Way, and that as in a dream he had till now been agitated to no purpose. He exclaimed, "But how marvelous and splendid! Just as the Master has taught without teaching, so I have truly heard without hearing. When hearing and teaching become one, all is wide and vast, oneness without words. Might I respectfully ask you, Venerable Master, by what title you would wish this above dialogue to come to be known?"

On becoming enlightened, Emmon also became aware of his delusions. These, without his troubling himself in any way about them, had now vanished of themselves. Delusions and faults do not have to be eradicated. They cease to be the moment they are realized. And enlightenment is not gaining something that from that moment onward becomes one's possession but is rather the shedding of all delusions, errors, and notions. As that, it is the voiding of everything that obscures truth and prevents it from revealing itself.

▓ 13 Master Nyuri just sat there for a while, without answering, and with shining eyes looked into the four directions. Then he chuckled and said to Emmon, "There are no words to express the profundity of the mysterious principle. It is ineffable. All your many questions were due to your speculative thinking and so were born in your heart. It is just like in a dream; though one may see all kinds of configurations, they all vanish on awakening.

So now you wish to make known these questions and answers to all and sundry and ask me to give them an expedient title. When even the last traces are vanished, call it *A Treatise on the Ceasing of Notions*."

"When even the last traces are gone" is when all the dirt of delusions has been washed off, together with the soap of the teaching, training, and enlightenment, and nothing at all remains—no smell of Zen, no ideology, no philosophy, no Buddha. Then the true nature functions freely and without any obstacles.

From *Novice to Master*:

AN ONGOING LESSON IN THE EXTENT
OF MY OWN STUPIDITY

By Soko Morinaga Roshi

The following section is adapted from Soko Morinaga's autobiography *Novice to Master: An Ongoing Lesson in the Extent of My Own Stupidity*, translated by Belenda Attaway Yamakawa and published by Wisdom Publications.

In this very personal, sometimes humorous and ironical reflection, Morinaga Roshi explains why and how, as a young man full of doubt and uncertainly, he chose to devote himself to the Zen monastic practice. In that practice he did not find immediate enlightenment, but through long hours of meditation, self inquiry, and the guidance and stimulus of his teacher Zuigan Roshi he came to see that he might, after all, let cease of his delusive thinking and recognize his own Buddhahood.

Preface

A WHILE AGO I gave a public lecture at a university. The speaker who preceded me talked for about an hour and a half, running over his allotted time. The break period between our talks was shortened, and I was called to the podium right away. Concerned for the audience, I opened by asking, "Did you all have time to urinate?"

Apparently this was not what the audience had expected to hear. Perhaps they were particularly surprised because the person standing before them, talking about pissing, was a monk. Everyone broke into hearty laughter.

Having started out on this note, I continued to press on. "Pissing is something that no one else can do for you. Only you can piss for yourself." This really broke them up, and they laughed even harder.

But you must realize that to say "You have to piss for yourself; nobody else can piss for you" is to make an utterly serious statement.

Long ago in China, there was a monk called Ken. During his training years, he practiced in the monastery of Ta-hui, but despite his prodigious efforts, he had not attained enlightenment. One day Ken's master ordered him to carry a letter to the far-off land of Ch'ang-sha. This journey, roundtrip, could easily take half a year. The monk Ken thought, "I don't have forever to stay in this hall practicing! Who's got time to go on an errand like this?" He consulted one of his seniors, the monk Genjoza, about the matter.

Genjoza laughed when he heard Ken's predicament. "Even while traveling you can still practice Zen! In fact, I'll come along with you"—and before long the two monks set out on their journey.

Then one day while the two were traveling, the younger monk suddenly broke into tears. "I have been practicing for many years, and I still haven't been able to attain anything. Now here I am roaming around the country on this trip; there's no way I am going to attain enlightenment this way," Ken lamented.

When he heard this, Genjoza, thrusting all his strength into his words, put himself at the junior monk's disposal: "I will take care of anything that I can take care of for you on this trip," he said. "But there are just five things that I cannot do in your place.

"I can't wear clothes for you. I can't eat for you. I can't shit for you. I can't piss for you. And I can't carry your body around and live your life for you."

It is said that upon hearing these words, the monk Ken suddenly awakened from his deluded dream and attained a great enlightenment, a great satori.

I hope that as you read this, you will realize that I am

not just talking about myself or about something that happened elsewhere. No, it is about your own urgent problems that I speak.

The Prospect
of My Own Death

IF I WERE to sum up the past forty years of my life, the time since I became a monk, I would have to say that it has been an ongoing lesson in the extent of my own stupidity. When I speak of my stupidity, I do not refer to something that is innate, but rather to the false impressions that I have cleverly stockpiled, layer upon layer, in my imagination.

Whenever I travel to foreign countries to speak, I am invariably asked to focus on one central issue: Just what is satori, just what is enlightenment? This thing called satori, however, is a state that one can understand only through experience. It cannot be explained or grasped through words alone.

By way of example, there is a proverb that says, "To have a child is to know the heart of a parent." Regardless of how a parent may demonstrate the parental mind to a child, that child cannot completely understand it. Only when children become parents themselves do they fully know the heart of a parent. Such an understanding can be likened to enlightenment, although enlightenment is far deeper still.

Because no words can truly convey the experience

of enlightenment, in this book I will instead focus on the essentials of Zen training, on my own path to awakening.

Let me start by saying that Zen training is not a matter of memorizing the wonderful words found in the sutras and in the records of ancient teachers. Rather, these words must serve as an impetus to crush the false notions of one's imagination. The purpose of practice is not to increase knowledge but to scrape the scales off the eyes, to pull the plugs out of the ears.

Through practice one comes to see reality. And although it is said that no medicine can cure folly, whatever prompts one to realize "I was a fool" is, in fact, just such a medicine.

It is also said that good medicine is bitter to the taste, and, sadly enough, the medicine that makes people aware of their own foolishness is certainly acrid. The realization that one has been stupid seems always to be accompanied by trials and tribulations, by setbacks and sorrows. I spent the first half of my own life writhing under the effects of this bitter medicine.

I was born in the town of Uozu in Toyama Prefecture, in central Japan. The fierce heat of World War II found me studying with the faculty of literature in Toyama High School, under Japan's old system of education. High school students had been granted formal reprieve from military duty until after graduation from university. When the war escalated, however, the order came down that students of letters were to depart for the front. Presumably students of science would go on to pursue courses of study in medicine or the natural sciences and thereby provide constructive cooperation in the war effort; students of literature, on the other hand, would merely read books, design arguments, and generally agitate the national spirit.

At any rate, we literature students, who came to be treated as nonstudents, had to take the physical examination for conscription at age twenty and then were marched, with no exceptions, into the armed forces. What is more, the draft age was lowered by one year, and as if under hot pursuit I was jerked unceremoniously into the army at the age of nineteen.

Of course we all know that we will die sooner or later. Death may come tomorrow, or it may come twenty or thirty years hence. Only our ignorance of just how far down the road death awaits affords us some peace of mind, enables us to go on with our lives. But upon passing the physical examination and waiting for a draft notice that could come any day, I found the prospect of my own death suddenly thrust before my eyes. I felt as though I were moving through a void day by day. Awake and in my sleep, I rehearsed the various ways in which I might die on the battlefield. But even though I found myself in a tumult of thoughts about death, there was no time for me to investigate the matter philosophically or to engage in any religious practice.

People who entered the army in those days rushed in headlong, fervently believing that ours was a just war, a war of such significance that they could sacrifice their lives without regret. Setting out in this spirit, we were armed with a provisional solution to the problem of death—or at least it was so in my case.

Among human beings, there are those who exploit and those who are exploited. The same holds true for relations among nations and among races. Throughout history, the economically developed countries have held dominion over the underdeveloped nations. Now, at last, Japan was rising to liberate herself from the chains of exploitation! This was a righteous fight, a meaningful fight! How could we begrudge our country this one small life, even if that life be smashed to bits? Such reckless rationalization allowed us to shut off our minds.

And so it was that we students set out in planes, armed only with the certainty of death and fuel for a one-way trip, with favorite works of philosophy or maybe a book about Buddha's Pure Land beside the control stick, certain to remain unread. Many lunged headlong at enemy ships; still many others were felled by the crest of a wave or knocked from the air before making that lunge.

Then, on August 15, 1945, came Japan's unconditional surrender. The war that everyone had been led to believe was so right, so just, the war for which we might gladly lay down our one life, was instead revealed overnight as a war of aggression, a war of evil—and those responsible for it were to be executed.

Nothing Is Certain

F OR BETTER or for worse, I returned from the army alive. Over a shortwave radio, an item extremely hard to come by in those days, I listened to the fate of the German leaders who had surrendered just a step ahead of the Japanese. When I heard the sentence that was read aloud at the Nuremberg Trials, "Death by hanging," the one word—*hanging*—lodged itself so tenaciously in my ears that I can still hear its echo. And then (perhaps through an American Occupation Forces policy?), a news film was shown. I saw this film at what is now the site of a department store, on the fifth floor of a crumbling cement block building that had only just narrowly escaped demolition in war-ravaged downtown Toyama.

In one scene, a German general was dragged to the top of a high platform and hanged before a great crowd that had assembled in the plaza. In another scene, the Italian leader Mussolini was lynched by a mob and then strung upside down on a wire beside the body of his lover. The film went on to show us how the dead bodies were subsequently dragged through the streets while the people hurled verbal abuse and flung rocks at them.

Wearing cast-off military uniforms, my classmates and I went back to school, one by one. We returned, young men unable to believe in anything and hounded by the question of right and wrong. Technically classes were resumed, but in reality no studying took place. If a teacher walked into the classroom, textbook under his arm, he would be asked to take a seat on the sidelines while members of the group who had just returned from the army took turns at the podium:

"Fortunately or not, we've been repatriated, and we're able to come back to school. But what we thought to be 'right' turned out overnight to be 'wrong.' We may live another forty or fifty years, but are we ever going to be able to believe in anything again—in a 'right' that can't be altered, in a 'wrong' that isn't going to change on us? If we don't resolve this for ourselves, no amount of study is ever going to help us build conviction in anything. Well, what do you fellows think?"

This went on day after day.

It so happened that in those days we had a philosophy teacher named Tasuku Hara. He later went on to become a professor in the philosophy department at Tokyo University. He was an excellent teacher, and I was sorry to hear that he died quite young. Anyway, one day this Professor Hara, who was like an older brother to us, stood up and insisted that we let him get a word in.

Taking the rostrum, he proceeded to talk to us, "Kant, the German philosopher in whose study I specialized, said this: We humans can spend our whole lives pondering the meaning of 'good' and 'evil,' but we will never be able to figure it out. The only thing that human beings can do is come up with a yardstick by which to measure good and evil."

"Looking at it this way," he continued, "if we use the yardstick of the Japanese, this war was a holy war, while by American criteria, it was a war of aggression. So your life's work is not to label this 'good' and that 'evil,' but to search for as useful a standard as you can find to apply anywhere you go on this earth. But this grand yardstick is not something you are going to come by in a day. Each of you will have to transcend time and place to find a standard that can have meaning to as many people as possible—and in order to do this, I suggest, first off, that you get on with your high school lessons!"

And so, with that kind advice, we resumed our classes. We did, however, also continue our self-indulgent theoretical debates. And I, for one, remained in a quandary over this question of good and evil; the problem had lodged itself deep in the back of my mind.

I think, in fact, that this was a dilemma of the times for Japan, common not only among young people like us, but among middle-aged and elderly people as well. We had completely lost sight of any ethical norm. I believe Japan had fallen into a state in which people scarcely knew what standards to apply even in raising their own children.

On top of all this, there were major changes in my own private affairs. To begin with, the year before the war ended, I had lost both of my parents in one blow: even as my mother was slipping away, my father suffered a cerebral hemorrhage and died the very next morning, August twenty-fourth, without having regained consciousness.

I have three older sisters, but all of them had already married and moved away. They were living in Moji, Shanghai, and Manchuria. Travel conditions being what they were in that day, none of my sisters was able to attend the funeral. As the sole survivor on the family registry, I was responsible for the funeral arrangements, which I completed within two days with help from relatives. Then, before I could settle any further affairs, I received my mustering order and found myself off to the army.

Upon my homecoming after the war had ended, I was greeted with the twin problems of property and inheritance taxes. I come from a long line of landowners, and the small amount of land we had was under tenancy in rice fields. My father had always told me, "There's nothing as dependable as land. Even if there's a fire, it won't burn. If there's a flood, it won't wash away. If a thief sneaks in, he can't cart it off on his back. No matter what else you do in this life, don't you let go of that land!"

It so happened, though, that through no action of my own, my family's land was lost to the government's agrarian reform program. So now with even this gone, what was left to believe in? All that I had ever thought to be certain had turned out to be uncertain.

The war I had thought was holy turned out to be evil. I had not expected my own parents to die so suddenly, and yet there they went, one right after the other. The insurance money that my father had set aside to provide for his children in the event that something should happen to him was subject to a freezing of funds, and not a cent was available for my use. And our ever-dependable land was now lost.

At the same time, prices were constantly on the rise. What could be bought for one yen one day cost ten yen the next, and before one knew it, a hundred-yen note was needed! It was practically unheard of in that time for students to hold part-time jobs, and consequently, I hadn't the slightest experience in using these hands and this body to earn wages. The problem of ethical standards aside, there was the very concrete economic question of how I was going to survive.

Looking back on myself in those days, I realize that it would not have been so curious if I had joined a gang of hooligans. Nor would it have been strange if I had committed suicide by hurling my body onto a railroad track. I woke up miserable every morning, and every day was as good as lost. Falling asleep in the worst of spirits, I would awaken to a new morning even darker.

This vicious cycle continued day after day, but somehow I managed to graduate from high school. However, as I had absolutely no inclination to enroll in university or to study anything at all, I went on to pass the days idly slouching around. Then, in the midst of that intense mental agony, I finally struck upon a realization: for as long as I could remember, I had done nothing but read books, acquire knowledge, churn up theories. The reason that I was now at a total loss for what to do with myself was, in the end, that I had never really used this body of mine in any kind of disciplined way.

The Encounter at Misery's End

So it was, through these mysterious causes and conditions, that I was led to knock at the gates of Zen temples. I still feel very grateful that, after calling at two or three temples, I was brought to Daishuin in Kyoto, where I still reside, to train under Zuigan Goto Roshi. Zuigan Roshi, formerly the abbot of Myoshinji and at that time the abbot of Daitokuji, was a truly great man.

I showed up at Roshi's door with long stringy hair, unkempt, with a towel hanging from my waist and heavy clogs on my feet. This great man's first words to me were, "Why have you come here?"

In reply, I rambled on for about an hour and a half, covering the particulars of my situation up to and including my present state. Roshi listened in silence, not attempting to insert so much as a single word.

When I had finished my exposition, he spoke, "Listening to you now, I can see that you've reached a point where there's nothing you can believe in. But there is no such thing as practice without believing in your teacher. Can you believe in me?

"If you can, I'll take you on right now, as you are. But

if you can't believe in me, then your being here is just a waste of time, and you can go right on back where you came from."

Zuigan Roshi, for his part, set forth in no uncertain terms from the very beginning the precept of believing wholeheartedly in one's teacher, but I was not sensible enough at that time to yield with a ready and honest affirmation.

Roshi was then seventy years old, and I told myself, "That foolish old man! So what if he is the head of Myoshinji or the head of Daitokuji. Lots of 'important' people in this world aren't worth much. If believing were so easy that I could just believe, unconditionally, in somebody I had just met for the first time, then wouldn't I have believed in something before I ever showed up here? Didn't I come here in the first place because I *don't* find it so easy to believe?"

All this ran through my mind, but I knew from the start that if I were to say it aloud, I would be told straightaway, "In that case, your being here is a waste of time. Go on home now."

Figuring that, even if my words were a lie, this man would have to let me stay if I spoke them, I said, "I believe in you. Please."

At that time, I had no idea of the weight of the words "I believe," but it was a lesson I was to be taught before the end of that very day.

There Is No Trash

"**F**OLLOW ME," directed the roshi, and he assigned me my first task: to clean the garden. Together with this seventy-year-old master, I went out to the garden and started sweeping with a bamboo broom. Zen temple gardens are carefully designed with trees planted to ensure that leaves will fall throughout the entire year; not only the maples in autumn but also the oaks and the camphors in spring regularly shed their foliage. When I first arrived, in April, the garden was full of fallen leaves.

The human being (or, my own mind, I should say) is really quite mean. Here I was, inside my heart denouncing this "old fool" and balking at the very idea of trusting so easily; yet, at the same time, I wanted this old man to notice me, and so I took up that broom and swept with a vengeance. Quite soon I had amassed a mountain of dead leaves. Eager to show off my diligence, I asked, "Roshi, where should I throw this trash?"

The words were barely out of my mouth when he thundered back at me, "There is no trash!"

"No trash, but...look here," I tried to indicate the pile of leaves.

"So you don't believe me! Is that it?"

"It's only that, well, where should I throw out these leaves?" That was all that was left for me to say.

"You don't throw them out!" he roared again.

"What should I do then?" I asked.

"Go out to the shed and bring back an empty charcoal sack," was his instruction.

When I returned, I found Roshi bent to the task of combing through the mountain of leaves, sifting so that the lighter leaves came out on top while the heavier sand and stones fell to the bottom. He then proceeded to stuff the leaves into the sack I had brought from the shed, tamping them down with his feet. After he had jammed the last leaves tightly into the sack, he said, "Take these to the shed. We'll use them to make a fire under the bath."

As I went off to the shed, I silently admitted that this sack of leaves over my shoulder was perhaps not trash, but I also told myself that what was left of that pile out there in the garden was clearly trash, and nothing but trash. I got back, though, only to find Roshi squatting over the remains of the leaf pile, picking out the stones. After he had carefully picked out the last stone, he ordered, "Take these out and arrange them under the rain gutters."

When I had set out the stones, together with the gravel that was already there, and filled in the spaces pummeled out by the raindrops, I found that not only were the holes filled but that my work looked rather elegant. I had to allow that these stones, too, failed to fall into the category of trash. There was still more, though: the clods of earth and scraps of moss, the last dregs. Just what could anyone possibly do with that stuff, I wondered.

I saw Roshi going about his business, gathering up these scraps and placing them, piece by piece, in the palm of his hand. He scanned the ground for dents and sinks; he filled them in with the clods of earth, which he then tamped down with his feet. Not a single particle remained of the mountain of leaves.

"Well?" he queried, "Do you understand a little bit better now? From the first, in people and in things, there is no such thing as trash."

This was the first sermon I ever heard from Zuigan Roshi. Although it did make an impression on me, unfortunately, I was not keen enough to attain any great awakening as a result of simply hearing these words.

From the first, in people and in things, there is no such thing as trash. These words point to the fundamental truth of Buddhism, a truth I could not as yet conceive in those days.

"Wonder of wonders! Intrinsically all living beings are buddhas, endowed with wisdom and virtue. Only because they cling to their delusive thinking do they fail to realize this." This was Shakyamuni Buddha's exclamation at the instant of his enlightenment. To put it in other words, all beings are, from the first, absolutely perfect, but because people are attached to deluded notions, they cannot perceive this innate buddha-nature.

In the classical Chinese sutras it is written that Shakyamuni said, "I attained buddhahood together with all the grasses, the trees, and the great earth."

In a split second, the mist before his eyes cleared, and Shakyamuni Buddha could see the true form of reality. "Up to now, I thought all beings in this world were living only in pain and misery, in deep unhappiness. But, in reality, aren't all beings, just as they are, living in buddhahood, living in a state of absolute perfection? And doesn't this apply not only to those who are healthy and sound of body but also to those who are blind, to those without hands, to the ones who are barely dragging themselves along? Isn't each and every one, just exactly as he or she presently is, a perfect and flawless being?" Awed and astonished, the Buddha called out in the voice of satori.

Every year, I go to Hokkaido to lecture, and one year, there was a woman present who asked to meet me after the talk. The young woman, an ardent believer in Christianity, had this to say: "Listening to your talk today, I could see that about all Buddhism tells us to do is throw away our desires. On the other hand, Christianity says, 'Ask, and it shall be given you. Seek, and you shall find. Knock, and the door shall be opened to you.' This teaching answers the hopes of young people like myself. What do you think about this, Roshi?"

I answered her with a question of my own. "Is that to say that no matter how you knock, no matter how you seek, you shall receive and the door will be opened to you? Is it not the case that unless one knocks and seeks in a way that is in accord with the heart of God, the door surely will not be opened, nor will one's desires be granted?"

I have heard the Christian teaching, "You devise your way, but God directs your steps"—you desire and choose and seek as you please, but it is God who decides whether or not your wishes are to be granted.

So, too, Buddhism does not say only to throw away all desire, to toss aside all seeking. It is especially in the Zen sect that we seek, that we knock at that door through a practice so intensive as to be like carving up our very bones. Buddhism points out, however, that after all the seeking, what we attain is the realization that what we have sought was always, from the first, already ours; after all the pounding away, we awaken to the fact that the door was already open before we ever began to knock.

So you see, Zuigan Roshi pointed out the most basic truth right from the start when he said, "From the first, in people and in things, there is no such thing as trash." Unfortunately, I did not understand him. I went on pretending to be a disciple who trusts his roshi, while inside my heart I criticized and resisted. To tell you the truth, I found almost everything he said irritating.

About the Author
and Translators

SOKO MORINAGA ROSHI was born in 1925. After graduating from high school, he entered Zen practice. He was ordained as a monk by Zuigan Goto in 1948. From 1949 through 1963, he trained in the monastery of Daitokuji and received the seal of Dharma transmission from Sesso Oda Roshi. While actively working in the lay community, delivering talks and writing books and articles, he served as the head of Hanazono University, the primary training university of the Rinzai sect, in Kyoto. He had a long-standing connection with the Buddhist Society of London and traveled there every year to participate in the summer school jointly sponsored by various Buddhist sects. Morinaga Roshi is the author of *Novice to Master*. He died in 1995.

MARTIN COLLCUTT is a professor of East Asian Studies and History at Princeton University, where he teaches Japanese intellectual and cultural history. He also has a particular interest in the introduction and development of the monastic practice in Japanese Rinzai Zen. In the 1960s he studied and practiced Zen in Japan and met Morinaga Roshi at Daishuin in Kyoto. Subsequently he served as Roshi's interpreter on some of his visits to the United States and England. His academic background in Japanese Zen and his personal and long-standing involvement with Morinaga Roshi and his teaching makes Professor Collcutt's informative introduction a valuable contribution to the understanding of this classic text.

URSULA JARAND practiced Zen in Kyoto under the guidance of Soko Morinaga Roshi for many years. Since 1994 she has been abbess of the Zen monastery Daishuin West in northern California. She has translated many Chinese Zen classics with commentaries by Soko Morinaga Roshi into German.

VEN. MYOKYO-NI, Irmgard Schloegl (1921–2007), was trained at Daitokuji monastery in Japan, where for twelve years she worked under two successive masters, Oda Sesso Roshi and Sojun Kannun Roshi. In 1977 she founded the Zen Centre in London. She was ordained in 1984 as the Ven. Myokyo-ni by Soko Morinaga Roshi and became abbess of the Zen Centre's two training temples, Shobo-an and Fairlight, over which she presided until her death in 2007. Ven. Myokyo-ni translated many important Zen classics from the Chinese and Japanese into English, such as *The Record of Rinzai* and *The Discourse on the Inexhaustible Lamp* (with Yoko Okuda). She also wrote many instructive books on Zen training—among them, *The Zen Way* and *Gentling the Bull*.

MICHELLE BROMLEY was a student of Venerable Myokyo-ni for many years. She is an independent editor and translator of Buddhist books into German and English.

About Wisdom Publications

WISDOM PUBLICATIONS is dedicated to offering works relating to and inspired by Buddhist traditions.

To learn more about us or to explore our other books, please visit our website at www.wisdompubs.org.

You can subscribe to our e-newsletter or request our print catalog online, or by writing to:

Wisdom Publications
199 Elm Street
Somerville, Massachusetts 02144 USA

You can also contact us at
617-776-7416,
or info@wisdompubs.org.

Wisdom is a nonprofit, charitable 501(c)(3) organization, and donations in support of our mission are tax deductible.

Wisdom Publications is affiliated with the Foundation for the Preservation of the Mahayana Tradition (FPMT).